Spectrum Te

Grade 2

Test Preparation for:

Reading
Language
Math

Program Authors:
Dale I. Foreman
S. Alan Cohen
Jerome D. Kaplan
Ruth Mitchell

Table of Contents

Published by McGraw-Hill Learning Materials, an imprint of McGraw-Hill Consumer Products.

1-57768-102-9

Spectrum Test Prep

The Program That Teaches Test-Taking Achievement

For over two decades, McGraw-Hill has helped students perform their best when taking standardized achievement tests. Over the years, we have identified the skills and strategies that students need to master the challenges of taking a standardized test. Becoming familiar with the test-taking experience can help ensure your child's success.

Spectrum Test Prep covers all test skill areas

Spectrum Test Prep contains the subject areas that are represented in the five major standardized tests. *Spectrum Test Prep* will help your child prepare for the following tests:

- California Achievement Tests® (CAT/5)
- Comprehensive Tests of Basic Skills (CTBS/4)
- Iowa Tests of Basic Skills® (ITBS, Form K)
- Metropolitan Achievement Test (MAT/7)
- Stanford Achievement Test (SAT/9)

Spectrum Test Prep provides strategies for success

Many students need special support when preparing to take a standardized test. *Spectrum Test Prep* gives your child the opportunity to practice and become familiar with:

- General test content
- The test format
- Listening and following standard directions
- Working in structured settings
- Maintaining a silent, sustained effort
- Using test-taking strategies

Spectrum Test Prep is comprehensive

Spectrum Test Prep provides a complete presentation of the types of skills covered in standardized tests in a variety of formats. These formats are similar to those your child will encounter when testing. The subject areas covered in this book include:

- Reading
- Language
- Math

Spectrum Test Prep gives students the practice they need

Each student lesson provides several components that help develop test-taking skills:

- An **Example,** with directions and sample test items
- A **Tips** feature, that gives test-taking strategies
- A Practice section, to help students practice answering questions in each test format

Each book gives focused test practice that builds confidence:

- A **Test Yourself** lesson for each unit gives students the opportunity to apply what they have learned in the unit.
- A **Test Practice** section gives students the experience of a longer test-like situation.
- A **Progress Chart** allows students to note and record their own progress.

Spectrum Test Prep is the first and most successful program ever developed to help students become familiar with the test-taking experience. Spectrum Test Prep can help to build self-confidence, reduce test anxiety, and provide the opportunity for students to successfully show what they have learned.

A Message to Parents and Teachers:

- **Standardized tests: the yardstick for your child's future**
  Standardized testing is one of the cornerstones of American education. From its beginning in the early part of this century, standardized testing has gradually become the yardstick by which student performance is judged. For better or worse, your child's future will be determined in great part by how well she or he performs on the standardized test used by your school district.

- **Even good students can have trouble with testing**
  In general, standardized tests are well designed and carefully developed to assess students' abilities in a consistent and balanced manner. However, there are many factors that can hinder the performance of an individual student when testing. These might include test anxiety, unfamiliarity with the test's format, or failing to understand the directions.

  In addition, it is rare that students are taught all of the material that appears on a standardized test. This is because the curriculum of most schools does not directly match the content of the standardized test. There will certainly be overlap between what your child learns in school and how he or she is tested, but some materials will probably be unfamiliar.

- **Ready to Test will lend a helping hand**
  It is because of the shortcomings of the standardized testing process that *Spectrum Test Prep* was developed. The lessons in the book were created after a careful analysis of the most popular achievement tests. The items, while different from those on the tests, reflect the types of material that your child will encounter when testing. Students who use *Spectrum Test Prep* will also become familiar with the format of the most popular achievement tests. This learning experience will reduce anxiety and give your child the opportunity to do his or her best on the next standardized test.

We urge you to review with your child the Message to Students and the feature "How to Use This Book" on pages 6-8. The information on these pages will help your child to use this book and develop important test-taking skills. We are confident that following the recommendations in this book will help your child to earn a test score that accurately reflects his or her true ability.

A Message to Students:

Frequently in school you will be asked to take a standardized achievement test. This test will show how much you know compared to other students in your grade. Your score on a standardized achievement test will help your teachers plan your education. It will also give you and your parents an idea of what your learning strengths and weaknesses are.

This book will help you do your best on a standardized achievement test. It will show you what to expect on the test and will give you a chance to practice important reading and test-taking skills. Here are some suggestions you can follow to make the best use of *Spectrum Test Prep*.

Plan for success

- You'll do your best if you begin studying and do one or two lessons in this book each week. If you only have a little bit of time before a test is given, you can do one or two lessons each day.
- Study a little bit at a time, no more than 30 minutes a day. If you can, choose the same time each day to study in a quiet place.
- Keep a record of your score on each lesson. The charts on pp. 160-162 of this book will help you do this.

On the day of the test . . .

- Get a good night's sleep the night before the test. Have a light breakfast and lunch to keep from feeling drowsy during the test.
- Use the tips you learned in *Spectrum Test Prep*. The most important tips are to skip difficult items, take the best guess when you're unsure of the answer, and try all the items.
- Don't worry if you are a little nervous when you take an achievement test. This is a natural feeling and may even help you stay alert.

How to Use This Book

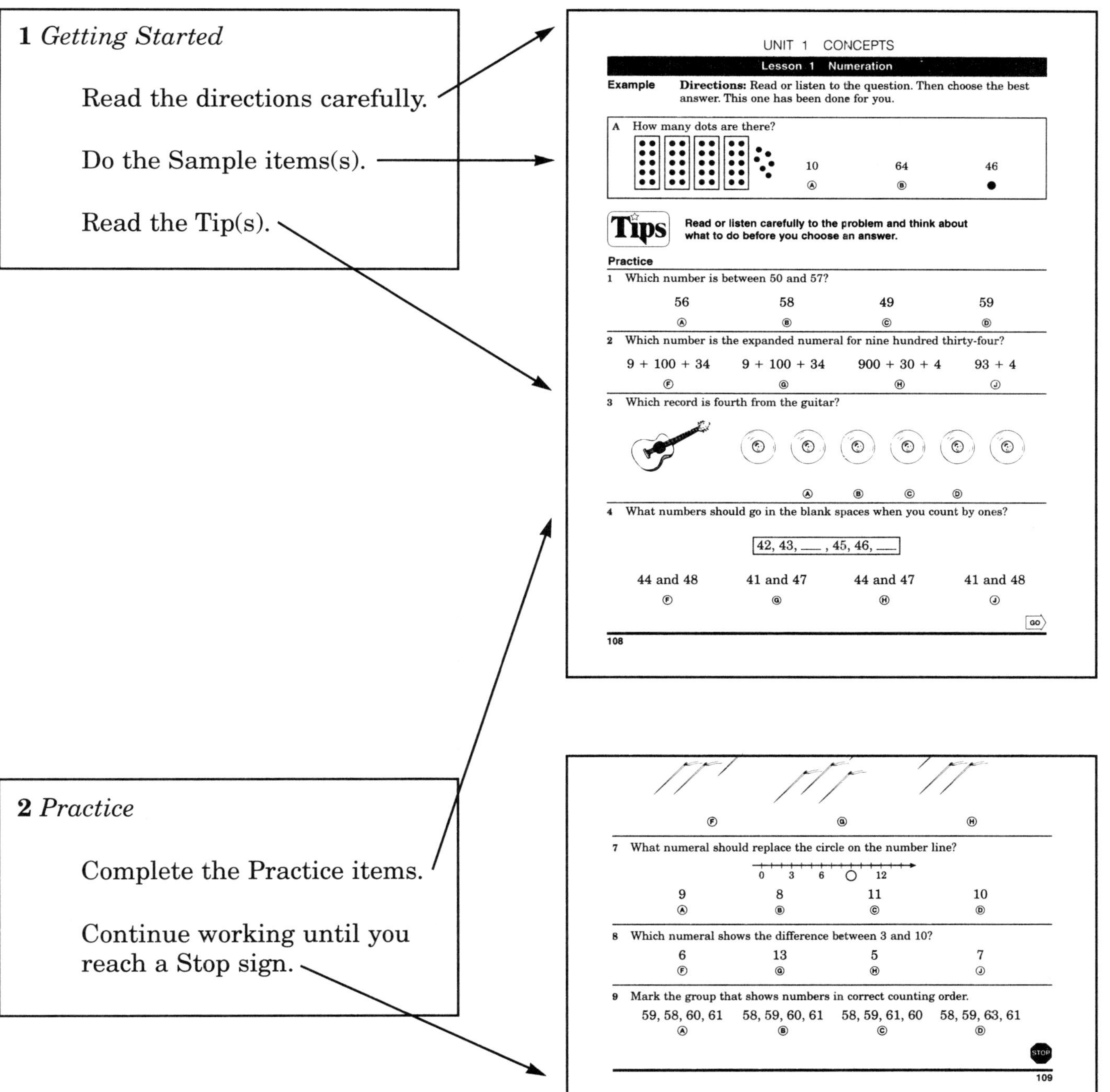

1 *Getting Started*

Read the directions carefully.

Do the Sample items(s).

Read the Tip(s).

UNIT 1 CONCEPTS

Lesson 1 Numeration

Example **Directions:** Read or listen to the question. Then choose the best answer. This one has been done for you.

A How many dots are there?

10 Ⓐ 64 Ⓑ 46 ●

Tips Read or listen carefully to the problem and think about what to do before you choose an answer.

Practice

1 Which number is between 50 and 57?

56 Ⓐ 58 Ⓑ 49 Ⓒ 59 Ⓓ

2 Which number is the expanded numeral for nine hundred thirty-four?

9 + 100 + 34 Ⓕ 9 + 100 + 34 Ⓖ 900 + 30 + 4 Ⓗ 93 + 4 Ⓙ

3 Which record is fourth from the guitar?

Ⓐ Ⓑ Ⓒ Ⓓ

4 What numbers should go in the blank spaces when you count by ones?

42, 43, ___ , 45, 46, ___

44 and 48 Ⓕ 41 and 47 Ⓖ 44 and 47 Ⓗ 41 and 48 Ⓙ

GO

108

2 *Practice*

Complete the Practice items.

Continue working until you reach a Stop sign.

Ⓕ Ⓖ Ⓗ

7 What numeral should replace the circle on the number line?

0 3 6 ○ 12

9 Ⓐ 8 Ⓑ 11 Ⓒ 10 Ⓓ

8 Which numeral shows the difference between 3 and 10?

6 Ⓕ 13 Ⓖ 5 Ⓗ 7 Ⓙ

9 Mark the group that shows numbers in correct counting order.

59, 58, 60, 61 Ⓐ 58, 59, 60, 61 Ⓑ 58, 59, 61, 60 Ⓒ 58, 59, 63, 61 Ⓓ

STOP

109

3 *Check It Out*

Check your answers by turning to the Answer Key at the back of the book.

Keep track of how you're doing by marking the number right on the Progress Charts on pages 160-162.

Mark the lesson you completed on the table of contents for each section.

Answer Key

Reading
Unit 1,
Word Analysis

Lesson 1–pg. 12
A A
B H
1 A
2 H
3 B
4 H
5 D
6 G
7 A
8 H

Lesson 2–pg. 13
A C
B G
1 A
2 G
3 A
4 F
5 C

Lesson 3–pg. 14
A C
B F
1 C
2 F
3 D
4 G
5 B
6 F

Lesson 4–pg. 15
A C
B F
C A
D G
1 B
2 F
3 C
4 G
5 C
6 G
7 C
8 G
9 C
10 G
11 C
12 F

Lesson 5–pg. 16
A B
B F
1 D
2 F
3 C
4 H
5 B
6 F
7 B
8 J

Lesson 6–pg. 17
A D
B H
1 A
2 G
3 B
4 H
5 D
6 H
7 A
8 G

Lesson 7–pgs. 18–21
E1 B
E2 F
E3 D
E4 H
E5 C
E6 G
E7 B
E8 H
1 C
2 F
3 B
4 F
5 C
6 J
7 B
8 H
9 A
10 G
11 A
12 H
13 A
14 G
15 A
16 H
17 C
18 F
19 C
20 F
21 D
22 G
23 A
24 G
25 A
26 G
27 C
28 F
29 C
30 F
31 B
32 F
33 B
34 G
35 A
36 H

Unit 2,
Vocabulary

Lesson 8–pg. 22
A C
B F
1 D
2 F
3 C
4 G

Lesson 9–pg. 23
A B
B H
1 C
2 J
3 C
4 F
5 D
6 G

Lesson 10–pg. 24
A B
B J
1 D
2 H
3 A
4 G
5 D
6 G

Lesson 11–pg. 25
A D
B F
1 C
2 G
3 A
4 J
5 B
6 J

Lesson 12–pg. 26
A B
B F
1 D
2 H
3 C
4 F
5 D
6 G

Lesson 13–pg. 27
A D
B J
1 B
2 F
3 D
4 H
5 B

Lesson 14–pgs. 28–31
E1 B
E2 J
E3 B
E4 H
E5 C
E6 F
E7 D
1 A
2 H
3 D
4 G
5 C
6 F
7 A
8 J
9 B
10 H
11 C
12 G
13 D
14 F
15 C
16 G
17 A
18 H
19 C
20 G
21 D
22 F
23 B
24 J
25 C
26 F
27 B
28 H
29 B
30 J

Unit 3,
Reading Comprehension

Lesson 15–pg. 32
A B
1 C

155

Reading Progress Chart

Circle your score for each lesson. Connect your scores to see how well you are doing.

Unit 1 Lesson 1	Lesson 2	Lesson 3	Lesson 4	Lesson 5	Lesson 6	Lesson 7	Unit 2 Lesson 8	Lesson 9	Lesson 10	Lesson 11	Lesson 12	Lesson 13	Lesson 14	Unit 3 Lesson 15	Lesson 16	Lesson 17	Lesson 18
8 7 6 5 4 3 2 1	5 4 3 2 1	6 5 4 3 2 1	12 11 10 9 8 7 6 5 4 3 2 1	8 7 6 5 4 3 2 1	8 7 6 5 4 3 2 1	36 35 34 33 32 31 30 29 28 27 26 25 24 23 22 21 20 19 18 17 16 15 14 13 12 11 10 9 8 7 6 5 4 3 2 1	4 3 2 1	6 5 4 3 2 1	6 5 4 3 2 1	6 5 4 3 2 1	6 5 4 3 2 1	5 4 3 2 1	30 29 28 27 26 25 24 23 22 21 20 19 18 17 16 15 14 13 12 11 10 9 8 7 6 5 4 3 2 1	6 5 4 3 2 1	4 3 2 1	14 13 12 11 10 9 8 7 6 5 4 3 2 1	15 14 13 12 11 10 9 8 7 6 5 4 3 2 1

Table of Contents
Reading

11

Skills

Reading

WORD ANALYSIS

Identifying initial consonant sounds
Identifying final consonant sounds
Matching vowel sounds
Recognizing initial sounds
Substituting initial sounds
Identifying words with matching vowel sounds
Identifying compound words
Recognizing suffixes
Recognizing contractions
Matching phonemes
Identifying contractions
Identifying compound words
Identifying root words
Identifying suffixes in words
Identifying rhyming words

VOCABULARY

Choosing a word to match a picture
Identifying the word to complete a sentence
Identifying synonyms
Identifying antonyms
Identifying words in sentence or paragraph contexts
Identifying multi-meaning words

READING COMPREHENSION

Understanding picture stories
Distinguishing between reality and fantasy
Drawing conclusions
Understanding characters
Differentiating between fact and opinion
Recognizing details
Making inferences
Making comparisons
Deriving word or phrase meaning
Understanding the author's purpose
Extending a story's meaning
Sequencing ideas
Choosing the best title for a story
Understanding the main idea
Understanding feelings

Language

LISTENING

Matching a picture to an oral or written scenario
Classifying a picture in response to an oral or written scenario
Identifying a word that does not fit an implied category.

LANGUAGE MECHANICS

Identifying the need for capital letters (proper nouns, beginning words) in sentences
Identifying the need for punctuation marks (period, question mark, exclamation point, comma) in sentences
Identifying the need for capital letters and punctuation marks in printed text

LANGUAGE EXPRESSION

Identifying the correct forms of nouns, pronouns, verbs, and adjectives
Recognizing double negatives
Identifying correctly formed sentences
Identifying the correct sentence to complete a paragraph
Identifying sentences that do not fit in a paragraph
Prewriting

SPELLING

Identifying correctly spelled words
Identifying incorrectly spelled words

STUDY SKILLS

Using a table of contents
Understanding a map
Using a picture dictionary
Alphabetizing words

Math

CONCEPTS

Associating numerals with number words
Comparing and ordering whole numbers
Counting using groupings of ten
Determining ordinal position
Estimating
Identifying fractional parts
Recognizing number sentences
Recognizing numerals 0-100
Recognizing numerals greater than 100
Recognizing visual and numeric patterns
Rounding
Sequencing
Skip counting
Solving number sentences
Understanding place value
Understanding terminology
Using a number line
Using expanded notation
Using operational symbols and properties

COMPUTATION

Adding whole numbers
Dividing whole numbers
Multiplying whole numbers
Subtracting whole numbers

APPLICATIONS

Estimating weight, size, and temperature
Finding perimeter
Forming solution sentences to oral and written word problems
Matching shapes
Reading a calendar
Recognizing plane and solid figures and their characteristics
Recognizing value of coins
Solving oral and written word problems
Telling time
Understanding congruence and symmetry
Understanding coordinate graphs
Understanding elapsed time
Understanding probability
Understanding spatial relations
Understanding tables and graphs
Understanding units of time
Using non-standard units of measurement
Using standard and metric units of measurement

Strategies

Adjusting to a structured setting
Reading and/or listening carefully
Utilizing test formats
Maintaining a silent, sustained effort
Locating questions and answer choices
Managing time effectively
Following oral and/or written directions
Considering every answer choice
Taking the best guess when unsure of the answer
Understanding unusual item formats
Working methodically
Comparing answer choices
Skipping difficult items and returning to them later
Recalling information about word structure
Staying with the first answer
Referring to a picture to answer a question
Identifying and using key words to find the answer
Using context to find the answer
Inferring word meaning from context
Trying out answer choices
Eliminating answer choices
Using logic and experience
Referring to a passage to answer questions
Reasoning from facts and evidence
Locating the correct answer
Indicating that an item has no mistakes
Following complex directions
Evaluating answer choices
Recalling the elements of a correctly formed sentence
Recalling the elements of a correctly formed paragraph
Avoiding overanalysis of answer choices
Referring to a reference source
Computing carefully
Converting problems to a workable format
Eliminating answer choices
Finding the answer without computing
Identifying and using key words, figures, and numbers
Identifying the best test-taking strategy
Listening to information presented orally
Marking the right answer as soon as it is found
Performing the correct operation
Saying answer choices to yourself

Table of Contents
Reading

Unit 1 Word Analysis

Unit 2 Vocabulary

Unit 3 Reading Comprehension

Unit 4 Test Practice

Lesson 1 Word Sounds

Examples **Directions:** Choose the best answer to each question.

What word begins with the same sound as shop? This one has been done for you.

A shake (A) start (B) check (C)

What word has the same sound as the underlined part? Practice on this one.

B lip write (F) choice (G) tin (H) train (J)

Tips **Listen carefully to the directions. Look at all the answer choices before choosing the one you think is correct.**

Practice

What word begins with the same sound as bread?

1 brush (A) block (B) price (C)

What word begins with the same sound as play?

2 prove (F) slip (G) plug (H)

What word ends with the same sound as bold?

3 felt (A) held (B) sand (C)

What word ends with the same sound as branch?

4 flash (F) rock (G) lunch (H)

What word has the same vowel sound as boot?

5 test (A) need (B) same (C) chew (D)

What word has the same vowel sound as head?

6 back (F) ten (G) leap (H) while (J)

What word has the same vowel sound as the underlined part?

7 log spot (A) roast (B) cloud (C) post (D)

What word has the same vowel sound as the underlined part?

8 fast main (F) race (G) man (H) near (J)

STOP

Examples **Directions:** Choose the best answer to each question.

A What word starts with the same sound as bring?

barn Ⓐ board Ⓑ brave ●

This one has been done for you.

B Which picture rhymes with the word in the box?

fell

Ⓕ Ⓖ Ⓗ

Practice on this one.

If you are not sure which answer is correct, take your best guess.

Practice

1 Which word begins with the same sound as usual?

unit Ⓐ until Ⓑ upset Ⓒ

2 Which word begins with the same sound as stretch?

slept Ⓕ strap Ⓖ search Ⓗ

3 Which word begins with the same sound as climb?

claim Ⓐ slide Ⓑ call Ⓒ

4 Which picture rhymes with the word in the box?

third

Ⓕ Ⓖ Ⓗ

5 Which picture rhymes with the word in the box?

late

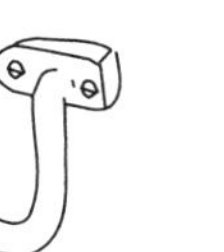

Ⓐ Ⓑ Ⓒ

STOP

Examples **Directions:** Which word has the same sound as the underlined

A This one has been done for you.	**B** Practice on this one.
trip (A) nice (B) oil (●C) stiff (D) mile	**mouse** (F) cloud (G) stole (H) road (J) human

Match the sound of the underlined letter or letters.

Look at each answer choice and say each answer choice to yourself.

Do numbers 1-6 the same way.

Practice

1 **burn**

Ⓐ juice
Ⓑ pound
Ⓒ first
Ⓓ ruin

2 **over**

Ⓕ close
Ⓖ bother
Ⓗ flood
Ⓙ cloth

3 **stripe**

Ⓐ bring
Ⓑ hair
Ⓒ chip
Ⓓ like

4 **reach**

Ⓕ pear
Ⓖ need
Ⓗ rest
Ⓙ hand

5 **strap**

Ⓐ tape
Ⓑ flat
Ⓒ roar
Ⓓ tear

6 **crow**

Ⓕ boast
Ⓖ clown
Ⓗ crust
Ⓙ would

STOP

Example A **Directions:** Which of these words is made up of two words?

basement Ⓐ carpet Ⓑ airplane ●

This one has been done for you. Do numbers 1-3 the same way.

Example C **Directions:** Which word is a contraction for have not?

haven't ● hasn't Ⓑ hadn't Ⓒ

This one has been done for you. Do numbers 7-9 the same way.

Pay careful attention to the directions. There are four kinds of items in this lesson.

Practice

1 drawer Ⓐ hotdog Ⓑ reason Ⓒ

2 horseback Ⓕ pottery Ⓖ rabbit Ⓗ

3 sparkle Ⓐ thirsty Ⓑ cowboy Ⓒ

Example B **Directions:** Choose the word that completes each sentence.

windy ● wind Ⓖ windier Ⓗ

The day was very ______.

This one has been done for you. Do numbers 4-6 the same way.

4 describes Ⓕ describing Ⓖ described Ⓗ

Sally was ______ her vacation.

5 trading Ⓐ trades Ⓑ trader Ⓒ

The ______ lived in a cabin by the road.

6 slowest Ⓕ slowly Ⓖ slower Ⓗ

The turtle moved more ______.

he will

7 he's Ⓐ he'd Ⓑ he'll Ⓒ

was not

8 weren't Ⓕ wasn't Ⓖ won't Ⓗ

does not

9 didn't Ⓐ don't Ⓑ doesn't Ⓒ

Example D Which word has the same sound as the underlined part?

match

then Ⓕ stem ● here Ⓗ

This one has been done for you. Do numbers 10-12 the same way.

10 **chip**

cost Ⓕ reach Ⓖ hit Ⓗ

11 **toy**

buy Ⓐ say Ⓑ oil Ⓒ

12 **defend**

wander Ⓕ lunch Ⓖ need Ⓗ

Examples **Directions:** Choose the words the contraction stands for.

		A	B	C	D
A	<u>you'll</u>	you tell	you will	you still	you fall

This one has been done for you. Do numbers 1-4 the same way.

Directions: Which word is made up of two words? This one has been done for you. Do numbers 5-8 the same way.

	F	G	H	J
B	goldfish	turtle	surprise	beautiful

If an item is too difficult, skip it and come back to it later, if you have time.

Practice

		A/F	B/G	C/H	D/J
1	<u>we've</u>	we love (A)	we save (B)	we prove (C)	we have (D)
2	<u>shouldn't</u>	should not (F)	should it (G)	should let (H)	should sit (J)
3	<u>they're</u>	they share (A)	they care (B)	they are (C)	they never (D)
4	<u>I'd</u>	I did (F)	I said (G)	I would (H)	I fed (J)

STOP

5	dinner (A)	armchair (B)	baby (C)	rocket (D)
6	screwdriver (F)	sudden (G)	worry (H)	different (J)
7	empty (A)	waterfall (B)	movement (C)	perfect (D)
8	person (F)	chicken (G)	really (H)	cookbook (J)

STOP

Examples **Directions:** What word shows the root or base word for the word on the left?

A	dangerous	dan	anger	gerous	danger
		Ⓐ	Ⓑ	Ⓒ	●

This one has been done for you. Do numbers 1-4 the same way.

Directions: What word shows the ending or suffix for the word on the left? This one has been done for you. Do numbers 5-8 the same way.

B	calling	ng	in	ing	ling
		Ⓕ	Ⓖ	●	Ⓙ

Stay with your first answer. Change it only if you are sure it is wrong and another answer is better.

Practice

1	kindest	kind Ⓐ	in Ⓑ	kin Ⓒ	dest Ⓓ
2	sounded	ded Ⓕ	sound Ⓖ	sou Ⓗ	ound Ⓙ
3	eaten	ten Ⓐ	eat Ⓑ	ate Ⓒ	ea Ⓓ
4	hopeful	hop Ⓕ	ful Ⓖ	hope Ⓗ	ope Ⓙ

STOP

5	actor	act Ⓐ	tor Ⓑ	cto Ⓒ	or Ⓓ
6	foolish	lish Ⓕ	olish Ⓖ	ish Ⓗ	fool Ⓙ
7	helpless	less Ⓐ	pless Ⓑ	help Ⓒ	ess Ⓓ
8	worker	or Ⓕ	er Ⓖ	wor Ⓗ	work Ⓙ

STOP

E1	Choose the word with the same beginning sound as the word on the left.				
	scream	slip (A)	scrap (B)	creep (C)	
E2	Choose the word that has the same vowel sound as the underlined part of the first word.				
	chin	list (F)	pine (G)	point (H)	pain (J)
E3	Find the word that is a compound word, a word that has two smaller words in it.				
	monkey (A)	bottom (B)	promise (C)	raindrop (D)	

Directions: Choose the word that begins or ends with the same sound as the one at the left.

1	clock	crush (A)	choose (B)	clip (C)
2	dry	drip (F)	deep (G)	dark (H)
3	ask	fish (A)	risk (B)	lost (C)
4	bent	hunt (F)	rock (G)	lunch (H)

Directions: Choose the word that has the same vowel sound as the one at the left.

5	rain	stand (A)	roar (B)	chase (C)	beach (D)
6	tough	pound (F)	mouth (G)	four (H)	must (J)
7	most	boil (A)	bone (B)	round (C)	soft (D)
8	line	stir (F)	chair (G)	fly (H)	miss (J)

STOP

Directions: Which word has the same beginning sound as the word shown?

9 crunch

cry	drip	climb
Ⓐ	Ⓑ	Ⓒ

10 aid

are	ape	and
Ⓕ	Ⓖ	Ⓗ

11 blade

blind	drill	train
Ⓐ	Ⓑ	Ⓒ

Directions: Choose the word that rhymes with the word shown.

12 here

heat	more	cheer
Ⓕ	Ⓖ	Ⓗ

13 friend

send	fresh	stand
Ⓐ	Ⓑ	Ⓒ

14 chest

chase	best	wash
Ⓕ	Ⓖ	Ⓗ

15 Which picture rhymes with the word in the box?

town

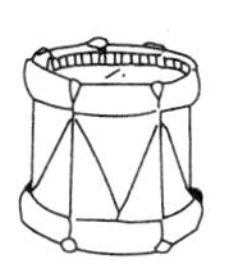

Ⓐ Ⓑ Ⓒ

16

wear

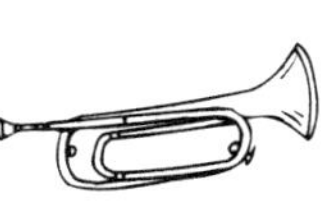

Ⓕ Ⓖ Ⓗ

17 Which picture shows a word with the same vowel sound as the word shown?

toast

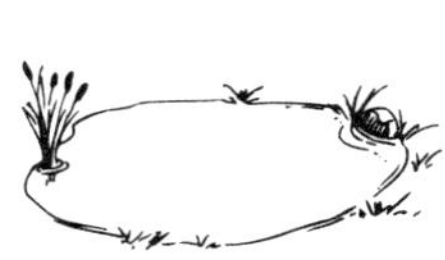

Ⓐ Ⓑ Ⓒ

18 slide

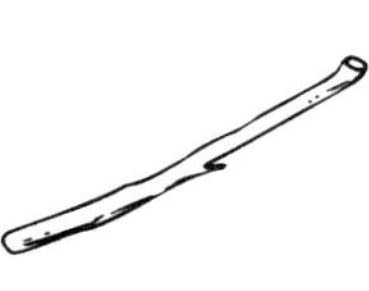

Ⓕ Ⓖ Ⓗ

STOP

Directions: Choose the word that has the same sound as the underlined part.

E4 **fool**

- (F) hope
- (G) bowl
- (H) boot ●
- (J) store

This one has been done for you.

Do numbers 19-22 the same way.

19 **raise**

- (A) lamp
- (B) trial
- (C) lake
- (D) rash

20 **need**

- (F) chief
- (G) next
- (H) bread
- (J) ever

21 **dot**

- (A) rope
- (B) broke
- (C) done
- (D) clock

22 **fuse**

- (F) crush
- (G) beauty
- (H) mouth
- (J) duck

STOP

Directions: Which word is the right contraction for the word shown?

E5 could not

couldn't	should've	shouldn't
(A) ●	(B)	(C)

This one has been done for you.

Do numbers 23-25 the same way.

23

isn't	wasn't	hasn't
(A)	(B)	(C)

24

she'd	she'll	she's
(F)	(G)	(H)

25

aren't	weren't	can't
(A)	(B)	(C)

Directions: Which word has the same sound as the underlined part of the word?

E6 **fine**

list	dry	chief
(F)	(G) ●	(H)

This one has been done for you.

Do numbers 26-28 the same way.

26 **friend**

scarf	frost	raft
(F)	(G)	(H)

27 **chair**

hour	near	rare
(A)	(B)	(C)

28 **damp**

red	team	poor
(F)	(G)	(H)

E7 Directions: Which vowel or vowels should go in the blank?

	o	a	u
b __ ll	Ⓐ	●	Ⓒ

This one has been done for you. Do numbers 29-30 the same way.

29

	i	a	u
tr __ ck	Ⓐ	Ⓑ	Ⓒ

30

	ou	oa	ue
h __ se	Ⓕ	Ⓖ	Ⓗ

31 Which of these words has a silent letter? Do number 32 the same way.

kind	knife	kept
Ⓐ	Ⓑ	Ⓒ

32

comb	clap	center
Ⓕ	Ⓖ	Ⓗ

33 Which ending should be added to the word in the box to make a new word?

help	ness	ful	ous
	Ⓐ	Ⓑ	Ⓒ

E8 Directions: What word has the same vowel sound as the one shown?

lake

talk	tan	take
Ⓕ	Ⓖ	Ⓗ

Do numbers 34-36 the same way.

34 root

for	food	found
Ⓕ	Ⓖ	Ⓗ

35 team

beach	bend	bale
Ⓐ	Ⓑ	Ⓒ

36 last

fear	fake	fast
Ⓕ	Ⓖ	Ⓗ

STOP

NUMBER RIGHT ______

Lesson 8 Picture Vocabulary

Examples **Directions:** Choose the word that matches the picture.

A

Ⓐ king
Ⓑ rule
● crown
Ⓓ royal

This one has been done for you.

B

Ⓕ messy
Ⓖ neat
Ⓗ sleepy
Ⓙ awake

Practice on this one.

Look at the picture and all the answer choices. Which word best matches the picture?

Do numbers 1-4 the same way.

Practice

1

Ⓐ date
Ⓑ month
Ⓒ clock
Ⓓ calendar

2

Ⓕ balance
Ⓖ swim
Ⓗ eat
Ⓙ clap

3

Ⓐ look
Ⓑ listen
Ⓒ crawl
Ⓓ carry

4

Ⓕ program
Ⓖ pennant
Ⓗ sports
Ⓙ crowd

STOP

Examples **Directions:** Choose the best answer.

A This one has been done for you.

Part of a shirt is a ….   Ⓐ zipper   ● collar   Ⓒ belt   Ⓓ brim

Practice on this one.

B To go someplace is to ….   Ⓕ prepare   Ⓖ raise   Ⓗ travel   Ⓙ enjoy

Key words in the item will help you find the answer.

Do numbers 1-6 the same way.

Practice

1 A sad face is a ….   Ⓐ smile   Ⓑ grin   Ⓒ frown   Ⓓ share

2 To buy something is to ….   Ⓕ find   Ⓖ return   Ⓗ repair   Ⓙ purchase

3 Something that just happened is ….   Ⓐ next   Ⓑ coming   Ⓒ recent   Ⓓ distant

4 To find something is to ….   Ⓕ discover   Ⓖ lose   Ⓗ replace   Ⓙ dismiss

5 A covering for a window is a ….   Ⓐ wall   Ⓑ door   Ⓒ carpet   Ⓓ curtain

6 Part of a leg is a ….   Ⓕ elbow   Ⓖ knee   Ⓗ finger   Ⓙ shoulder

Examples **Directions:** Look at the underlined word in each sentence. Which word is a synonym for that word?

A Tina likes to <u>carve</u> the turkey.

Ⓐ eat
● cut
Ⓒ cook
Ⓓ stuff

This one has been done for you.

B This is my <u>usual</u> lunch.

Ⓕ favorite
Ⓖ special
Ⓗ brother's
Ⓙ normal

Practice on this one.

Use the meaning of the sentence to help you find the meaning of the word.

Do numbers 1-6 the same way.

Practice

1 George read the <u>entire</u> book.

Ⓐ exciting
Ⓑ library
Ⓒ science
Ⓓ whole

2 It was a <u>pleasant</u> day.

Ⓕ stormy
Ⓖ cold
Ⓗ nice
Ⓙ hot

3 Can you <u>recall</u> her name?

Ⓐ remember
Ⓑ write
Ⓒ spell
Ⓓ forget

4 Let's <u>shout</u> to my sister.

Ⓕ run
Ⓖ yell
Ⓗ write
Ⓙ jog

5 The grass is <u>damp</u>.

Ⓐ dry
Ⓑ green
Ⓒ high
Ⓓ moist

6 This is the <u>finish</u> of the race.

Ⓕ start
Ⓖ end
Ⓗ hard part
Ⓙ middle

STOP

Lesson 11 Antonyms

Examples **Directions:** Look at the underlined word in each sentence. Which word is the antonym to that word?

A The story made Walt grin.

Ⓐ angry
Ⓑ smile
Ⓒ yawn
● frown

This one has been done for you.

B Is that your brother?

Ⓕ sister
Ⓖ cousin
Ⓗ uncle
Ⓙ aunt

Practice on this one.

Look for the answer that means the opposite of the underlined word.

Skip difficult items and come back to them later.

Do numbers 1-6 the same way.

Practice

1 Her room is always so neat.

Ⓐ colorful
Ⓑ dark
Ⓒ messy
Ⓓ bright

2 Who will raise the flag?

Ⓕ buy
Ⓖ lower
Ⓗ find
Ⓙ unpack

3 The fans in the stands were calm.

Ⓐ excited
Ⓑ sad
Ⓒ disappointed
Ⓓ loud

4 Cara likes to spend her money.

Ⓕ waste
Ⓖ share
Ⓗ donate
Ⓙ save

5 Allan felt weak after the race.

Ⓐ tired
Ⓑ strong
Ⓒ hungry
Ⓓ surprised

6 Don't stretch your sweater.

Ⓕ fold
Ⓖ lose
Ⓗ damage
Ⓙ shrink

Examples **Directions:** Choose the word that fits in the blanks.

A The team had a hard_______ . The players were tired.

Ⓐ reason Ⓒ bench
❷ game Ⓓ base

This one has been done for you.

B Our dog got out of the yard. We had to _______ him around the block until he came home.

Ⓕ chase Ⓗ call
Ⓖ feed Ⓙ pet

Practice on this one.

If you aren't sure of the answer, try each answer choice in the blank.

Practice

1 The stream was too deep. We had to _______ across it.

Ⓐ visit Ⓒ stand
Ⓑ carry Ⓓ jump

2 On Saturday, we helped my aunt build a _______ around the garden.

Ⓕ floor Ⓗ wall
Ⓖ row Ⓙ nest

The highway was **(3)** . People were traveling to the **(4)** to enjoy the sunshine and warm water.

3 Ⓐ long Ⓒ crowded
Ⓑ wide Ⓓ beginning

4 Ⓕ beach Ⓗ school
Ⓖ store Ⓙ town

Janet's room has a large _______ . When she looks out, she can see the _______ buildings of the city.

5 Ⓐ carpet Ⓒ shelf
Ⓑ desk Ⓓ window

6 Ⓕ wild Ⓗ open
Ⓖ tall Ⓙ lost

STOP

Lesson 13 Multi-Meaning Words

Examples **Directions:** Some words have more than one meaning. Choose the word that will make sense in both blanks.

A We _______ go to the park on Saturday.
A _______ of soup is on the shelf.

Ⓐ will Ⓒ cup
Ⓑ may ● can

This one has been done for you. Do numbers 1-3 the same way.

B **Directions:** Read the sentence. Then choose the best answer to the question. This one has been done for you. Do numbers 4-5 the same way.

She lost her ring.

In which sentence does the word ring mean the same thing as in the sentence above?

Ⓕ A glass can be made to ring.
Ⓖ We joined hands to form a ring.
Ⓗ Did you ring the doorbell?
● A ring was on her finger.

Remember, the correct answer must make sense in both blanks or match the sentence in the box.

Practice

1 My father _______ for work at eight o'clock.
The _______ fell from the tree.

Ⓐ dance Ⓒ play
Ⓑ leaves Ⓓ catch

2 We can _______ here for a while.
The _______ of the wood is in the yard.

Ⓕ rest Ⓗ pile
Ⓖ stop Ⓙ sit

3 Whose _______ is it to wash the dishes?
You should _______ when you come to the stop sign.

Ⓐ chance Ⓒ wait
Ⓑ look Ⓓ turn

4 **Pick up your clothes.**

In which sentence does the word pick mean the same thing as in the sentence above?

Ⓕ Use a pick to break up the dirt.
Ⓖ This apple is the pick of the crop.
Ⓗ Jay volunteered to pick up trash.
Ⓙ We'll pick you up at noon.

5 **Do you miss your friends?**

In which sentence does the word miss mean the same thing as in the sentence above?

Ⓐ Miss Wilson owns the store.
Ⓑ I miss spending time at the lake.
Ⓒ Jane didn't miss any games.
Ⓓ We'll lose if you miss the ball.

E1 Directions: Choose the word that matches the picture.

Ⓐ hold
❷ point
Ⓒ drop
Ⓓ catch

This one has been done for you. Do numbers 1-3 the same way.

1

Ⓐ study
Ⓑ play
Ⓒ argue
Ⓓ visit

2

Ⓕ angry
Ⓖ lazy
Ⓗ funny
Ⓙ noisy

3

Ⓐ feel
Ⓑ sense
Ⓒ listen
Ⓓ view

STOP

Directions: Choose the best answer.

E2 To jump is to ....
Ⓕ fall Ⓖ step Ⓗ skip ❶ leap
This one has been done for you.

Do numbers 4-6 the same way.

4 To tell someone what to do is to .... Ⓕ call Ⓖ order Ⓗ offend Ⓙ contact

5 Something that has been fixed is .... Ⓐ repeated Ⓑ released Ⓒ repaired Ⓓ received

6 A large container for water is a .... Ⓕ barrel Ⓖ chest Ⓗ basket Ⓙ carton

STOP

Directions: Choose the word that means the same as the words shown.

E3 To speak quietly

Ⓐ attend Ⓑ whisper (filled) Ⓒ catch Ⓓ trust

This one has been done for you. Do numbers 7-9 the same way.

7 a jungle animal

Ⓐ lion Ⓑ robin Ⓒ sheep Ⓓ mouse

8 something you write on

Ⓕ radio Ⓖ bell Ⓗ chair Ⓙ paper

9 to discover

Ⓐ drop Ⓑ find Ⓒ give Ⓓ pull

STOP

Choose the word that is an antonym for the underlined word.

E4 <u>straight</u> path

Ⓕ take Ⓖ reject Ⓗ crooked (filled) Ⓙ realize

This one has been done for you. Do numbers 10-15 the same way.

10 food on a <u>plate</u>

Ⓕ wall Ⓖ bridge Ⓗ dish Ⓙ song

11 <u>easy</u> test

Ⓐ long Ⓑ surprise Ⓒ simple Ⓓ take

12 <u>hurry</u> home

Ⓕ leave Ⓖ rush Ⓗ nice Ⓙ answer

STOP

13 <u>open</u> door

Ⓐ wide Ⓑ pretty Ⓒ quiet Ⓓ closed

14 arrive <u>sooner</u>

Ⓕ later Ⓖ when Ⓗ still Ⓙ happier

15 <u>always</u> remember

Ⓐ slowly Ⓑ quickly Ⓒ never Ⓓ nearby

STOP

What word best fits in the blank?

16 The _______ of the store helped me find the coat.

Ⓕ friend Ⓖ manager Ⓗ customer Ⓙ driver

Do this one the same way.

17 I had to _______ to my friend because the noise was so loud.

Ⓐ shout Ⓑ remind Ⓒ listen Ⓓ go

STOP

Directions: Look at the underlined word. Which choice defines the word?

E5 To combine is to —

- Ⓐ separate
- Ⓑ search for
- ● mix together
- Ⓓ buy

This one has been done for you.

E6 Practice on this one.

My arm was aching after I bumped it. Aching means —

- Ⓕ sore
- Ⓖ strong
- Ⓗ weak
- Ⓙ wet

E7 Directions: Read each sentence. Then choose the best answer to the question. Do numbers 22 and 23 the same way.

Place the book on the shelf.

In which sentence does the word place mean the same thing as in the sentence above?

- Ⓐ Meet me at John's place.
- Ⓑ Which place was the most fun?
- Ⓒ Annie held my place in line.
- Ⓓ Did you place the cup on the desk?

Do numbers 18-21 the same way.

18 To pretend is to —

- Ⓕ join
- Ⓖ argue
- Ⓗ make believe
- Ⓙ lose something

19 A section is a —

- Ⓐ town
- Ⓑ path
- Ⓒ part
- Ⓓ vegetable

20 We had a wonderful feast at Thanksgiving. A feast is a —

- Ⓕ hike
- Ⓖ large meal
- Ⓗ telephone call
- Ⓙ game

21 A storm interrupted the game. Interrupted means —

- Ⓐ improved
- Ⓑ replaced
- Ⓒ started
- Ⓓ stopped

22

Be sure to tie the knot tightly.

In which sentence does the word tie mean the same thing as in the sentence above?

- Ⓕ Tie the string around the papers.
- Ⓖ This tie goes with that shirt.
- Ⓗ The game ended in a tie.
- Ⓙ We used a railroad tie for a step.

23

We'll have to brush the dirt off.

In which sentence does the word brush mean the same thing as in the sentence above?

- Ⓐ This brush is too large for that job.
- Ⓑ Joy will brush the leaves away.
- Ⓒ We had a close brush with a bear.
- Ⓓ The ball flew into the heavy brush.

STOP

Choose the word that fits in the blank. Do numbers 24-30 the same way.

The **(24)** was dirty after we walked on it. I got the **(25)** and swept it clean.

24 Ⓕ table Ⓖ dish Ⓗ room Ⓙ floor

25 Ⓐ towel Ⓑ bag Ⓒ broom Ⓓ hose

The newspaper had an **(26)** story. A new business was **(27)** to our town.

26 Ⓕ important Ⓖ often Ⓗ empty Ⓙ ending

27 Ⓐ leaving Ⓑ moving Ⓒ building Ⓓ standing

---

28 That _______ is too small for my finger.
Did you hear the telephone _______ ?

Ⓕ call Ⓖ glove Ⓗ ring Ⓙ sound

29 Rob wanted to _______ the mail before he left.
Cindy paid for the food with a _______ .

Ⓐ read Ⓑ check Ⓒ dollar Ⓓ send

30 The _______ swam to the middle of the pond.
Be sure to _______ your head when you walk under the tree.

Ⓕ fish Ⓖ move Ⓗ girl Ⓙ duck

STOP

Lesson 15 Picture Comprehension

Example **Directions:** Look at the picture. Then choose the word that fits in the blank.

A The board has a ______ in it.

Ⓐ wood ● hole Ⓒ nail Ⓓ scratch

This one has been done for you. Do numbers 1-6 the same way.

Look back at the picture when you answer a question.

Practice

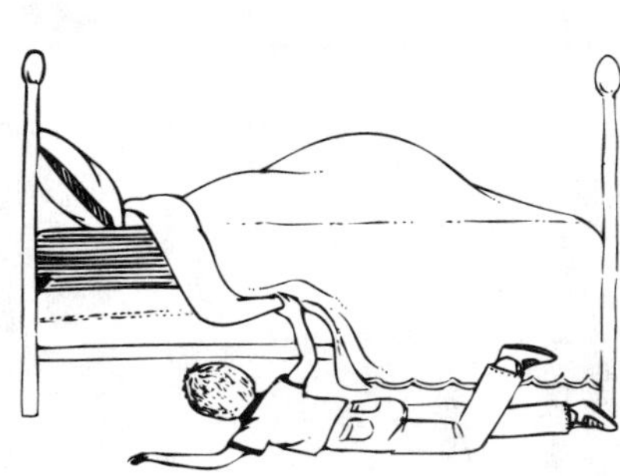

1 Roger is looking under the ______ .

Ⓐ table Ⓑ chair Ⓒ bed Ⓓ dresser

2 His dog, Tiger, is ______ somewhere.

Ⓕ hiding Ⓖ running Ⓗ begging Ⓙ barking

3 Roger will be ______ when he finds Tiger.

Ⓐ early Ⓑ late Ⓒ sad Ⓓ happy

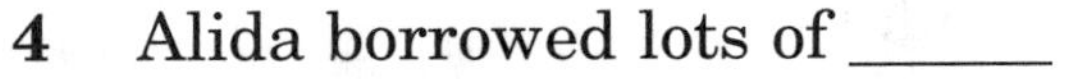

4 Alida borrowed lots of ______ .

Ⓕ shoes Ⓖ books Ⓗ videos Ⓙ toys

5 She is waiting for the ______ to open.

Ⓐ movie Ⓑ bank Ⓒ store Ⓓ library

6 Alida will ______ the books to the library.

Ⓕ carry Ⓖ sell Ⓗ return Ⓙ lend

Example **Directions:** Read each sentence. Which one describes something that could not happen?

A
Ⓐ We watched the ants as they worked.
Ⓑ They never stopped working.
Ⓒ One of them looked up at us.
● It said, "Why aren't you working like us?"

This one has been done for you. Do numbers 1-4 the same way.

Pay attention to the question. Think about what could and could not happen.

Practice

1
Ⓐ Sandy took a walk.
Ⓑ She followed a path through a field of tall grass.
Ⓒ Suddenly a horse flew over her head.
Ⓓ Sandy decided to turn around and go home.

2
Ⓕ Zak the cat liked to sit in the window and watch the birds.
Ⓖ He drew pictures of them using crayons.
Ⓗ Sometimes Zak would fall asleep in the window.
Ⓙ Once he almost fell out of the window when a bird flew by.

3
Ⓐ The driver stopped the car and got out.
Ⓑ The car suddenly turned into an elephant.
Ⓒ The elephant looked at the driver.
Ⓓ Then the elephant danced down the street.

4
Ⓕ "It looks like a hot summer," the tree said.
Ⓖ "Yes," answered the grass, "a very hot summer."
Ⓗ The tree took a long drink of water from the stream.
Ⓙ The fish in the stream continued swimming.

Example **Directions:** Read or listen to the story. Choose the best answers to the questions about the story.

Marty got his tools, some nails, and a few pieces of wood. He looked at the plans and picked up a piece of wood. Then he began to work.

A Marty will probably be using a —

- Ⓐ hammer (filled)
- Ⓑ bat
- Ⓒ fishing rod
- Ⓓ kite

This one has been done for you. Do numbers 1-14 the same way.

Look back at the story to answer the questions.

Practice

"There's nothing to do," said Nicole. "I'm bored."

"Take a look at this," answered her father. "It's a video about Sign Language. Maybe you can learn how to talk to people who are deaf."

Nicole put the video in the player and turned it on. The lady on the video showed her many signs and taught her the alphabet. The first sign she learned was "help." After that, she learned many other signs.

The next day, when she went to school, she told her friends what she had learned. They were excited. After school, some of them went to Nicole's house. They watched the video and learned Sign Language. Nicole was glad her father had a good idea.

1 Who had a good idea?

- Ⓐ Nicole
- Ⓑ Nicole's mother
- Ⓒ Nicole's father
- Ⓓ Nicole's teacher

2 Which of these is a fact?

- Ⓕ The lady on the video was nice.
- Ⓖ Nicole learned Sign Language.
- Ⓗ Everyone likes Sign Language.
- Ⓙ The video about Sign Language is the best.

GO

Most very large cities have one or more famous museums. Museums are places where people can go to learn about art, science, nature, history, or other interesting subjects. Museums are surprisingly popular. More people go to museums than to professional sporting events.

Art museums are usually quiet places. People go there to study paintings, statues, and other forms of art. In an art museum, pictures are often grouped together in collections because they were made by the same artist or were painted in a similar style.

Science museums are more active places. They have exhibits that show how things work and explain the mysteries of science. People like science museums because they get to try many wonderful experiments.

Natural history museums show the many wonders of nature, such as rocks, gems, animals, and plants. Almost every natural history museum has a display of dinosaurs. This is usually the most popular part of the museum because children and adults love all kinds of dinosaurs.

3 **Where are famous museums most often found?**

Ⓐ In foreign countries

Ⓑ In large cities

Ⓒ In the suburbs

4 **Which of these would be found in a natural history museum?**

Ⓕ An exhibit about wild horses

Ⓖ The paintings of Georgia O'Keeffe

Ⓗ An exhibit about rockets

5 **What is a difference between art and science museums?**

Ⓐ Science museums are quieter

Ⓑ Art museums are more crowded

Ⓒ Art museums are quieter

6 **In this story, what is a "collection"?**

Ⓕ A group of famous pictures

Ⓖ A group of things that were found

Ⓗ A group of similar pictures

GO

Butterfly of Thailand

My friends and family call me Butterfly. It is my nickname. My real name is Kamon, and I live in Thailand. This is a country far away, near China.

My home is on the water, on a canal called a klong. We go everywhere by small boats called sampans. We even go to school on a boat. Farmers take their fruits and vegetables to market by boat. They sell their fruits and vegetables at a place called the Floating Market. This is like a supermarket on the water. It is open every day for people to buy and sell food and other things.

We wash our clothes and take baths in the klong. Every child learns to swim. We do not drink or cook with the water from the klong. We catch rain water in large jars for that.

My family eats rice at almost every meal. We also have fish or meat, fruit, and vegetables. Most of our dinners are spicy and peppery.

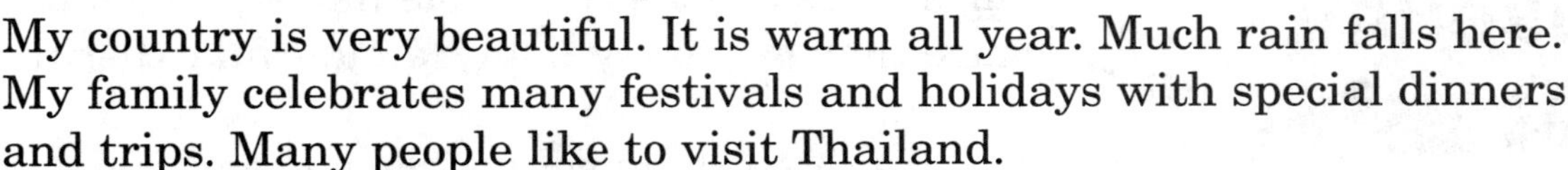

My country is very beautiful. It is warm all year. Much rain falls here. My family celebrates many festivals and holidays with special dinners and trips. Many people like to visit Thailand.

7 This story was written mainly to —

- Ⓐ tell what a place looks like.
- Ⓑ show how to do something.
- Ⓒ solve a problem.
- Ⓓ tell about how people live.

8 How does the family celebrate holidays?

- Ⓕ By going to the Floating Market
- Ⓖ With a meal and a trip
- Ⓗ By resting
- Ⓙ By playing sports

9 What is the best way to learn more about Thailand?

- Ⓐ Read a book about Thailand
- Ⓑ Look up Thailand in the dictionary
- Ⓒ Eat food from Thailand
- Ⓓ Visit a canal

10 In Thailand, a canal is called a —

- Ⓕ sampan.
- Ⓖ Floating Market.
- Ⓗ klong.
- Ⓙ Kamon.

GO

Did you ever iron a sandwich?

One rainy Saturday, Kim and Barbara were playing at Kim's house. Kim's mother was ironing. "What's for lunch, Mom?" asked Kim. "We want something different."

"How would you like to make cheese sandwiches on the ironing board?" Kim's mother asked.

"You can't cook on an ironing board, silly," said Kim.

"Yes you can, if you follow these directions," said Kim's mother.

Ironing Board Sandwiches

For each sandwich:

Toast two slices of bread in the toaster.
Place a slice of cheese between them.
Wrap the sandwich in aluminum foil.
Hold the hot iron on one side for a minute.
Turn the sandwiches over, and "iron" the other side.
Unwrap carefully. The foil will be hot.

While the girls were toasting the bread and making sandwiches, Kim's mother heated tomato soup. Barbara poured milk. The three of them had a delicious lunch.

11 How long should you heat each side of the sandwich with the iron?

Ⓐ One minute

Ⓑ Two minutes

Ⓒ Five minutes

12 After the bread was toasted, the next thing they did was to —

Ⓕ cook tomato soup.

Ⓖ add cheese.

Ⓗ pour milk.

13 What is a good name for this story?

Ⓐ "Grilled Cheese Sandwiches"

Ⓑ "Lunch on a Rainy Day"

Ⓒ "Ironing a Sandwich"

14 Barbara and Kim were —

Ⓕ surprised that you could iron a sandwich.

Ⓖ not very good at following directions.

Ⓗ happy that it was raining.

STOP

Example **Directions:** Read or listen to the story. Choose the best answers to the questions about the story.

The Statue of Liberty was a gift to the United States from the people of France. It stands tall in New York harbor as a sign of hope.

A The Statue of Liberty is in —

Ⓐ France Ⓑ Holland Ⓒ New York Ⓓ Washington

Directions: Look at the picture. Then read or listen to the sentences. Choose the word that best completes the sentence.

1 Lucy and her brother, Noah, are at the ______ .

Ⓐ beach Ⓑ store Ⓒ zoo Ⓓ library

2 Noah enjoys looking at the ______ .

Ⓕ animals Ⓖ fish Ⓗ trees Ⓙ flowers

3 The children ______ zoo chow to the monkeys.

Ⓐ receive Ⓑ remove Ⓒ send Ⓓ toss

Directions: Read or listen to the story. Choose the best answers to the questions about the story.

"Let's take a walk down to the pond," said Aunt Lisa. "There are some things I want you to see."

Aaron and I followed Aunt Lisa down the path through the tall grass. When we reached the pond, she told us to be quiet and pointed to a rock near the bank.

"This is a frog we call 'Rocky' because he always sits on that rock. If you look near the weeds, you can see one of our fish."

The fish was very still. Suddenly, it swam to the surface and gulped a fly that had landed in the water. We were all surprised at how fast the fish moved. Aunt Lisa said that both the frogs and the fish in the pond eat bugs.

4 Which of these did the children see first?

Ⓕ

Ⓖ

Ⓗ

STOP

Look at these sentences. Which one describes something that couldn't really happen?

5 Ⓐ The shoe store was having a big sale.

Ⓑ Dora and Armen decided to buy new shoes.

Ⓒ They took the bus to the mall and walked to the store.

Ⓓ All the shoes were dancing in the store window.

Directions: Read or listen to the story. Choose the best answers to the questions about the story.

Too Many Shoes?

Did you ever wonder why there are so many different kinds of shoes? The answer is simple. Your feet are very important, and having the right shoes lets you work and play safely and comfortably.

Probably the most famous shoes are cowboy boots. They are known around the world. The pointy toes of cowboy boots let you put your feet easily into the stirrups of a saddle. The big heels keep your feet from slipping out of the stirrups.

The strangest shoes are probably ski boots. They are so stiff you can't walk in them well. They attach to skis and help to protect your feet and legs.

6 **What is this story mostly about?**

Ⓕ shoes

Ⓖ ski boots

Ⓗ cowboy boots

Ⓙ comfort

7 **Stirrups are part of a —**

Ⓐ horse.

Ⓑ saddle.

Ⓒ ski.

Ⓓ shoe.

GO

Directions: Read or listen to the story. Choose the best answers to the questions about the story.

Rainbows and Clouds

This special dessert will take a little time to make, but your family will enjoy it. You'll need 3 packages of gelatin mix in 3 different colors, water, whipped topping, a measuring cup, a spoon, and a large pan or dish. You could use strawberry gelatin for red, lime for green, and lemon for yellow.

Mix one package of gelatin. Heat one cup of water in the microwave for a minute. Stir in the gelatin powder. Mix well. Add one cup of cold water. Stir again. Pour this into the pan or dish. It will be a thin layer. Put it in the refrigerator for about an hour or until it has set.

Mix the second package of gelatin the same way. Carefully pour it over the first layer in the dish. Let it chill for an hour or until it has set.

Mix the third package. Pour it over the other layers. Chill for an hour or longer. Be sure it is firm, not runny.

Cut the rainbow gelatin into squares. Carefully lift each square out of the dish. Set it on a plate. Add a "cloud" of whipped topping on one corner. This recipe makes several servings.

8 After you mix the hot water, cold water, and gelatin powder, you should —

- Ⓕ add more cold water.
- Ⓖ add the whipped topping.
- Ⓗ pour it into the pan or dish.
- Ⓙ cut it into squares.

9 The different colored layers will look like a —

- Ⓐ rainbow.
- Ⓑ cloud.
- Ⓒ dish of ice cream.
- Ⓓ flower garden.

10 This dessert will take a long time to make because—

- Ⓕ each of the layers must freeze into ice before adding the next layer.
- Ⓖ the dessert has to bake in the oven for a long time.
- Ⓗ the gelatin and water have to be mixed for a very long time.
- Ⓙ the layers of gelatin have to chill and set.

11 A good time to make this dessert is —

- Ⓐ in the morning before school.
- Ⓑ on a rainy Saturday afternoon.
- Ⓒ at night before going to bed.
- Ⓓ just before you leave on a trip.

GO

Directions: Read or listen to the story. Choose the best answers to the questions about the story.

Oak trees are among the most important trees in the United States. They grow in many places around the country and range in size from a small bush to a giant tree over a hundred feet tall. Oaks grow wild in forests, and they are also a popular tree for home gardens.

The wood of oak trees is used for building furniture. It is a hard wood that has a beautiful grain. People like oak furniture because it is sturdy and looks pretty. Antique furniture that is made of oak is very valuable even though it might be several hundred years old.

Oak trees produce a nut called an acorn. Animals and birds love to eat acorns. Squirrels and jays often bury acorns and come back for them later. They sometimes forget where they buried the acorns, and from these buried acorns grow more oak trees.

12 What is this story mostly about?

Ⓕ Oak trees

Ⓖ Important trees

Ⓗ Using trees

13 In this story, what does "antique" mean?

Ⓐ Something very sturdy

Ⓑ Something very old

Ⓒ Something very beautiful

14 How do jays help oak trees?

Ⓕ They build their nests in oak trees and lay their eggs.

Ⓖ They love to eat acorns.

Ⓗ They bury acorns so more trees will grow.

15 What is an acorn most like?

Ⓐ The root of a sunflower.

Ⓑ The leaf of an apple tree

Ⓒ The seed of a tomato plant

Name and Answer Sheet

To the Student:

These tests will give you a chance to put the tips you have learned to work.

A few last reminders . . .

- Be sure you understand all the directions before you begin each test. You may ask the teacher questions about the directions if you do not understand them.
- Work as quickly as you can during each test.
- When you change an answer, be sure to erase your first mark completely.
- You can guess at an answer or skip difficult items and go back to them later.
- Use the tips you have learned whenever you can.
- It is OK to be a little nervous. You may even do better.

Now that you have completed the lessons in this unit, you are on your way to scoring high!

STUDENT'S NAME

LAST											FIRST						MI
A	A	A	A	A	A	A	A	A	A	A	A	A	A	A	A	A	A
B	B	B	B	B	B	B	B	B	B	B	B	B	B	B	B	B	B
C	C	C	C	C	C	C	C	C	C	C	C	C	C	C	C	C	C
D	D	D	D	D	D	D	D	D	D	D	D	D	D	D	D	D	D
E	E	E	E	E	E	E	E	E	E	E	E	E	E	E	E	E	E
F	F	F	F	F	F	F	F	F	F	F	F	F	F	F	F	F	F
G	G	G	G	G	G	G	G	G	G	G	G	G	G	G	G	G	G
H	H	H	H	H	H	H	H	H	H	H	H	H	H	H	H	H	H
I	I	I	I	I	I	I	I	I	I	I	I	I	I	I	I	I	I
J	J	J	J	J	J	J	J	J	J	J	J	J	J	J	J	J	J
K	K	K	K	K	K	K	K	K	K	K	K	K	K	K	K	K	K
L	L	L	L	L	L	L	L	L	L	L	L	L	L	L	L	L	L
M	M	M	M	M	M	M	M	M	M	M	M	M	M	M	M	M	M
N	N	N	N	N	N	N	N	N	N	N	N	N	N	N	N	N	N
O	O	O	O	O	O	O	O	O	O	O	O	O	O	O	O	O	O
P	P	P	P	P	P	P	P	P	P	P	P	P	P	P	P	P	P
Q	Q	Q	Q	Q	Q	Q	Q	Q	Q	Q	Q	Q	Q	Q	Q	Q	Q
R	R	R	R	R	R	R	R	R	R	R	R	R	R	R	R	R	R
S	S	S	S	S	S	S	S	S	S	S	S	S	S	S	S	S	S
T	T	T	T	T	T	T	T	T	T	T	T	T	T	T	T	T	T
U	U	U	U	U	U	U	U	U	U	U	U	U	U	U	U	U	U
V	V	V	V	V	V	V	V	V	V	V	V	V	V	V	V	V	V
W	W	W	W	W	W	W	W	W	W	W	W	W	W	W	W	W	W
X	X	X	X	X	X	X	X	X	X	X	X	X	X	X	X	X	X
Y	Y	Y	Y	Y	Y	Y	Y	Y	Y	Y	Y	Y	Y	Y	Y	Y	Y
Z	Z	Z	Z	Z	Z	Z	Z	Z	Z	Z	Z	Z	Z	Z	Z	Z	Z

SCHOOL

TEACHER

FEMALE ○ MALE ○

BIRTH DATE

MONTH	DAY		YEAR	
JAN ○	0	0		0
FEB ○	1	1		1
MAR ○	2	2		2
APR ○	3	3		3
MAY ○		4		4
JUN ○		5	5	5
JUL ○		6	6	6
AUG ○		7	7	7
SEP ○		8	8	8
OCT ○		9	9	9
NOV ○				
DEC ○				

GRADE

1 2 3

PART 1 WORD ANALYSIS

E1 A B C D	4 F G H J	16 F G H J	28 F G H J	40 F G H J
E2 F G H J	5 A B C D	17 A B C D	29 A B C D	41 A B C D
E3 A B C D	6 F G H J	18 F G H J	30 F G H J	
E4 F G H J	7 A B C D	19 A B C D	31 A B C D	
E5 A B C D	8 F G H J	20 F G H J	32 F G H J	
E6 F G H J	9 A B C D	21 A B C D	33 A B C D	
E7 A B C D	10 F G H J	22 F G H J	34 F G H J	
E8 F G H J	11 A B C D	23 A B C D	35 A B C D	
E9 A B C D	12 F G H J	24 F G H J	36 F G H J	
1 A B C D	13 A B C D	25 A B C D	37 A B C D	
2 F G H J	14 F G H J	26 F G H J	38 F G H J	
3 A B C D	15 A B C D	27 A B C D	39 A B C D	

PART 2 VOCABULARY

E1 A B C D	5 A B C D	16 F G H J	27 A B C D	38 F G H J
E2 F G H J	6 F G H J	17 A B C D	28 F G H J	39 A B C D
E3 A B C D	7 A B C D	18 F G H J	29 A B C D	40 F G H J
E4 F G H J	8 F G H J	19 A B C D	30 F G H J	41 A B C D
E5 A B C D	9 A B C D	20 F G H J	31 A B C D	42 F G H J
E6 F G H J	10 F G H J	21 A B C D	32 F G H J	43 A B C D
E7 A B C D	11 A B C D	22 F G H J	33 A B C D	44 F G H J
1 A B C D	12 F G H J	23 A B C D	34 F G H J	45 A B C D
2 F G H J	13 A B C D	24 F G H J	35 A B C D	46 F G H J
3 A B C D	14 F G H J	25 A B C D	36 F G H J	47 A B C D
4 F G H J	15 A B C D	26 F G H J	37 A B C D	

PART 3 READING COMPREHENSION

E1 A B C D	5 A B C D	11 A B C D	17 A B C D
E2 F G H J	6 F G H J	12 F G H J	18 F G H J
1 A B C D	7 A B C D	13 A B C D	19 A B C D
2 F G H J	8 F G H J	14 F G H J	
3 A B C D	9 A B C D	15 A B C D	
4 F G H J	10 F G H J	16 F G H J	

Part 1 · Word Analysis

Directions: Choose the best answer to each question.

These have been done for you.

E1 Which word has the same beginning sound as chase?

creek	cloud	chip
Ⓐ	Ⓑ	●

E2 Which word has the same vowel sound as the underlined word?

use	up	mouse	burn	soup
	Ⓕ	Ⓖ	Ⓗ	●

E3 Which word is a compound word, a word made from two words?

overcoat	chicken	follow	wooden
●	Ⓑ	Ⓒ	Ⓓ

1 Which word has the same beginning sound as free?

friend	flake	first
Ⓐ	Ⓑ	Ⓒ

2 Which word has the same beginning sound as stripe?

swing	stretch	shrink
Ⓕ	Ⓖ	Ⓗ

3 Which word has the same ending sound as truck?

black	much	milk
Ⓐ	Ⓑ	Ⓒ

4 Which word has the same ending sound as cart?

harm	past	sort
Ⓕ	Ⓖ	Ⓗ

5 Which word has the same vowel sound as choice?

cow	joy	found	tooth
Ⓐ	Ⓑ	Ⓒ	Ⓓ

6 Which word has the same vowel sound as beach?

bend	desk	pile	piece
Ⓕ	Ⓖ	Ⓗ	Ⓙ

7 What word has the same vowel sound as the underlined part?

learn	reach	here	firm	loose
	Ⓐ	Ⓑ	Ⓒ	Ⓓ

8 What word has the same vowel sound as the underlined part?

cow	bowl	couch	own	roast
	Ⓕ	Ⓖ	Ⓗ	Ⓙ

STOP

Directions: Which word is a compound word, a word made from two other words?

E4 This one has been done for you.

music (F) · seaweed (G, filled) · instead (H)

Do numbers 9-11 the same way.

9 shadow (A) · between (B) · paintbrush (C)

10 wildcat (F) · correct (G) · report (H)

11 baseball (A) · farmer (B) · practice (C)

Directions: Which word should be used to fill in the blank?

E5 Darryl ______ a picture.

drawing (A) · draws (B, filled) · draw (C)

This one has been done for you. Do numbers 12-14 the same way.

12 I have many ______.

friends (F) · friend (G) · friendlier (H)

13 My parents are concerned about my ______.

safer (A) · safe (B) · safety (C)

14 It is ______ raining.

harder (F) · hardly (G) · hardy (H)

Directions: Choose the contraction that stands for the words.

E6 was not

wasn't (F, filled) · isn't (G) · can't (H)

This one has been done for you. Do numbers 15-17 the same way.

15 where is

where's (A) · where'd (B) · where'll (C)

16 had not

haven't (F) · hasn't (G) · hadn't (H)

17 he would

he'd (A) · he's (B) · he'll (C)

Directions: Choose the word that has the same sound as the underlined part.

E7 best (b underlined)

dirt (A) · band (B, filled) · rest (C)

This one has been done for you. Do numbers 18-20 the same way.

18 meet (ee underlined)

mend (F) · read (G) · heart (H)

19 stand (s underlined)

ship (A) · slow (B) · step (C)

20 hard (ar underlined)

bird (F) · drop (G) · dish (H)

STOP

E8 Directions: Choose the answer that has the same vowel sound as the underlined part.

clear

- Ⓕ bread
- Ⓖ steer (filled)
- Ⓗ lend
- Ⓙ stare

This one has been done for you. Do numbers 21-28 the same way.

E9 Practice on this one.

joy

- Ⓐ yellow
- Ⓑ joke
- Ⓒ stony
- Ⓓ boil

21 **truth**

- Ⓐ rough
- Ⓑ just
- Ⓒ group
- Ⓓ dusty

22 **chair**

- Ⓕ chalk
- Ⓖ high
- Ⓗ chip
- Ⓙ dare

23 **police**

- Ⓐ nice
- Ⓑ steep
- Ⓒ line
- Ⓓ pole

24 **row**

- Ⓕ slow
- Ⓖ cow
- Ⓗ dew
- Ⓙ love

25 **cage**

- Ⓐ paid
- Ⓑ can't
- Ⓒ bag
- Ⓓ tiger

26 **step**

- Ⓕ steer
- Ⓖ these
- Ⓗ let
- Ⓙ tip

27 **poor**

- Ⓐ rode
- Ⓑ stone
- Ⓒ tour
- Ⓓ open

28 **start**

- Ⓕ stare
- Ⓖ march
- Ⓗ hurt
- Ⓙ stay

STOP

Which words does the contraction stand for?

29	couldn't	could not (A)	could get (B)	could sit (C)	could next (D)
30	aren't	are hot (F)	are late (G)	are not (H)	are meant (J)
31	haven't	have it (A)	have ever (B)	have not (C)	have even (D)

STOP

Which word is a compound word?

32	famous (F)	horseshoe (G)	amazing (H)	owner (J)
33	future (A)	report (B)	pirate (C)	classroom (D)
34	travel (F)	doorknob (G)	whether (H)	explore (J)

STOP

Which word is the root word of the word on the left?

35	endless	ndle (A)	en (B)	end (C)	less (D)
36	oldest	old (F)	dest (G)	lde (H)	est (J)
37	nicely	cely (A)	nice (B)	nic (C)	cely (D)

STOP

Which is the suffix of the word on the left?

38	sleepy	epy (F)	sleep (G)	y (H)	leepy (J)
39	landed	ed (A)	and (B)	anded (C)	land (D)
40	builder	build (F)	uil (G)	der (H)	er (J)
41	floating	ating (A)	ing (B)	float (C)	oat (D)

STOP

Directions: Choose the word that matches the picture.

E1 This one has been done for you.

Ⓐ pot
Ⓑ pan
● bowl
Ⓓ dish

Do numbers 1-3 the same way.

1

Ⓐ await
Ⓑ listen
Ⓒ arrange
Ⓓ compute

2

Ⓕ damaged
Ⓖ strong
Ⓗ healthy
Ⓙ replaced

3

Ⓐ retrieve
Ⓑ revolve
Ⓒ repeat
Ⓓ resist

STOP

Directions: Which word has the same beginning sound as the one shown?

E2 This one has been done for you.
step

shell	stump	spell
Ⓕ	Ⓖ	Ⓗ

Do numbers 4-6 the same way.

4 elbow

east	ocean	enter
Ⓕ	Ⓖ	Ⓗ

5 touch

there	table	thank
Ⓐ	Ⓑ	Ⓒ

6 inside

stripe	island	improve
Ⓕ	Ⓖ	Ⓗ

7 Which word has the same vowel sound as roof?

boot	road	loud
Ⓐ	Ⓑ	Ⓒ

8 Which word has the same vowel sound as block?

rope	stop	black
Ⓕ	Ⓖ	Ⓗ

STOP

Directions: Choose the word that best fits the description.

E3 to move upward

Ⓐ answer
● climb
Ⓒ reach
Ⓓ dent

This one has been done for you. Do numbers 9-11 the same way.

9 something you drink

Ⓐ fruit
Ⓑ glass
Ⓒ wood
Ⓓ juice

10 something you put on a stamp

Ⓕ box
Ⓖ pen
Ⓗ stamp
Ⓙ deliver

11 to misplace something

Ⓐ lose
Ⓑ store
Ⓒ purchase
Ⓓ lend

Directions: Find the word that means about the same as the underlined word. Mark your choice.

12 <u>finish</u> a job

Ⓕ seek
Ⓖ end
Ⓗ reach
Ⓙ open

13 <u>cool</u> weather

Ⓐ hot
Ⓑ normal
Ⓒ chilly
Ⓓ late

14 <u>see</u> birds

Ⓕ hear
Ⓖ catch
Ⓗ follow
Ⓙ watch

Directions: Find the word that means the opposite of the underlined word.

E4 <u>wet</u> towel

Ⓕ dry
Ⓖ damp
Ⓗ heavy
Ⓙ real

Do numbers 15-17 the same way.

15 <u>fat</u> fish

Ⓐ thin
Ⓑ large
Ⓒ swimming
Ⓓ fast

16 <u>lead</u> a crowd

Ⓕ join
Ⓖ feel
Ⓗ follow
Ⓙ among

17 <u>tall</u> person

Ⓐ short
Ⓑ high
Ⓒ nice
Ⓓ old

Directions: Find the word that best completes each sentence.

18 The _______ from Centerville and Mildale is rough.

Ⓕ town
Ⓖ pole
Ⓗ house
Ⓙ road

19 You will need the _______ to climb up on the roof.

Ⓐ floor
Ⓑ ladder
Ⓒ bell
Ⓓ room

STOP

Directions: Choose the word that is closest in meaning to the underlined word.

E5 This one has been done for you.
To celebrate is to —

- Ⓐ have a party (filled in)
- Ⓑ play a game
- Ⓒ go to sleep
- Ⓓ find something

E6 Practice on this one.
The crane landed in the pond. A crane is a kind of —

- Ⓕ fish
- Ⓖ frog
- Ⓗ turtle
- Ⓙ bird

E7

The seal swam into the waves.

In which sentence does the word seal mean the same thing as in the sentence above?

- Ⓐ The king's seal was on the scroll.
- Ⓑ Seal the letter before mailing it.
- Ⓒ Did you visit the seal tank?
- Ⓓ The plastic bag has a tight seal.

Do numbers 20-32 the same way.

20 Dull means not —

- Ⓕ funny
- Ⓖ sad
- Ⓗ happy
- Ⓙ bright

21 A frame goes around a —

- Ⓐ picture
- Ⓑ field
- Ⓒ room
- Ⓓ car

22 Imaginary means —

- Ⓕ real
- Ⓖ made up
- Ⓗ unusual
- Ⓙ rare

23 A dome is a kind of —

- Ⓐ wall
- Ⓑ roof
- Ⓒ floor
- Ⓓ room

24 Confused means —

- Ⓕ a little sad
- Ⓖ late
- Ⓗ mixed up
- Ⓙ early

25 If something is worn it is —

- Ⓐ not new
- Ⓑ cheap
- Ⓒ lost
- Ⓓ not here

26 A lodge is a —

- Ⓕ field
- Ⓖ lake
- Ⓗ building
- Ⓙ mountain

27 Pleasant means —

- Ⓐ nice
- Ⓑ huge
- Ⓒ soft
- Ⓓ colorful

GO

28 Horses like to snort with their noses. To snort is to —

Ⓕ run Ⓗ make a noise

Ⓖ jump Ⓙ wear a saddle

29 It was an ordinary day in which nothing happened. Ordinary is —

Ⓐ busy Ⓒ strange

Ⓑ normal Ⓓ boring

30 Minora attended the Miller School. Attended means —

Ⓕ lived near Ⓗ liked

Ⓖ left Ⓙ went to

31 The band leader used a baton. A baton is a kind of —

Ⓐ stick Ⓒ tape

Ⓑ record Ⓓ piano

32 All that was left was the core of the apple. Core means —

Ⓕ outside Ⓗ skin

Ⓖ inside Ⓙ stem

Directions: Read or listen to the sentence. Choose the best answer to the question.

33

Whose turn is it?

In which sentence does the word turn mean the same thing as in the sentence above?

Ⓐ Shonto made a right turn.

Ⓑ Turn the radio on, please.

Ⓒ Remember to turn the page.

Ⓓ My turn comes after Winnie's.

34

The back of the room is noisy.

In which sentence does the word back mean the same thing as in the sentence above?

Ⓕ We will go back to the lake soon.

Ⓖ Milk is in the back of the store.

Ⓗ Can you back up a little?

Ⓙ Allen hurt his back swimming.

35

Give me a hand with this box.

In which sentence does the word hand mean the same thing as in the sentence above?

Ⓐ Karen cut her hand on a shell.

Ⓑ We were able to lend them a hand.

Ⓒ The crowd gave the team a hand.

Ⓓ Hand me that hammer, please.

STOP

36 Which picture matches the sentence?

Both monkeys were hanging upside-down.

Ⓕ

Ⓖ

Ⓗ

37 Do this one the same way.

The students visited an old fort.

Ⓐ

Ⓑ

Ⓒ

Look at the picture. Choose the answer that best completes each sentence.

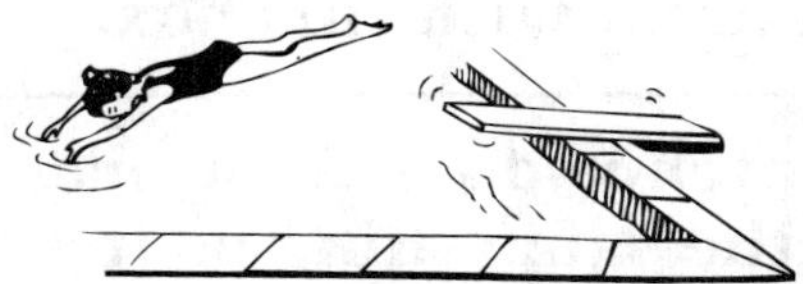

38 Christa likes to go to the ______ .

Ⓕ ocean Ⓖ river Ⓗ pool Ⓙ lake

39 She enjoys ______ most of all.

Ⓐ diving Ⓑ running Ⓒ jumping Ⓓ swimming

40 After she dives, Christa will climb ______ the pool.

Ⓕ into Ⓖ through Ⓗ around Ⓙ out of

STOP

Directions: Choose the words that best fit in the blanks.

We followed a **(41)** through the woods. It lead us to a cool **(42)** with many fish.

41 Ⓐ tree Ⓑ field Ⓒ shadow Ⓓ path

42 Ⓕ farm Ⓖ stream Ⓗ clearing Ⓙ bench

The stars **(43)** in the night sky. The whole city was **(44)** with a blanket of snow.

43 Ⓐ stopped Ⓑ twinkled Ⓒ lasted Ⓓ above

44 Ⓕ covered Ⓖ crowded Ⓗ empty Ⓙ alone

STOP

---

45 During the _______ , the leaves turn beautiful colors.
Be careful not to _______ down the steps.

Ⓐ day
Ⓑ climb
Ⓒ fall
Ⓓ weather

46 Can you help me find a _______ that matches this shirt?
You will need string to _______ that package.

Ⓕ coat
Ⓖ tie
Ⓗ close
Ⓙ hat

47 Coal comes from a _______ that goes far underground.
The brown dog is _______ .

Ⓐ mine
Ⓑ hole
Ⓒ hers
Ⓓ friendly

STOP

Part 3 Reading Comprehension

Directions: Read the sentences. Which one tells something that could really happen?

E1 Ⓐ The cars in the parking lot lined themselves up.

● Emmy Lou walked past the parking lot.

Ⓒ The cars followed her down the street.

Ⓓ Then they began singing to her.

This one has been done for you.

Directions: Find the best answer to the question. Mark the space for your answer.

E2 Aunt Nora works in a funny place, a lighthouse. She makes sure that ships don't run into the rocks. Every night she turns the light on so sailors will see it.

Aunt Nora works near the —

Ⓕ mountains. Ⓗ desert.

Ⓖ mall. Ⓙ ocean.

Directions: Read the sentences. Find the sentence that tells something that could not really happen. Do numbers 1 and 2 the same way.

1 Ⓐ Mr. Munch, the rabbit, decided to build a house of bricks.

Ⓑ Rollie read a book about where animals live.

Ⓒ Turtles have shells, so they bring their homes with them.

Ⓓ Birds build nests of sticks and twigs.

2 Ⓕ One of the things I like to do is hike in the mountains.

Ⓖ There are many trails near the town where I live.

Ⓗ I always hike with friends or my family.

Ⓙ The mountains move to get out of the way when I hike.

STOP

Directions: Read the sentences. Find the sentence that tells something that could really happen. Do numbers 3 and 4 the same way.

3 Ⓐ People jumped out of the television and became real.

Ⓑ Carl listens to the news on the radio with his family.

Ⓒ The radio started singing to the television people.

Ⓓ The people from the television danced around the room.

4 Ⓕ "What a wonderful day for a picnic," said the blanket.

Ⓖ "I hope no ants bother us," answered the basket.

Ⓗ Harry and Sally drove to the park.

Ⓙ The ants held up a sign that said, "Welcome."

Directions: Read or listen to the story. Choose the best answers to the questions about the story.

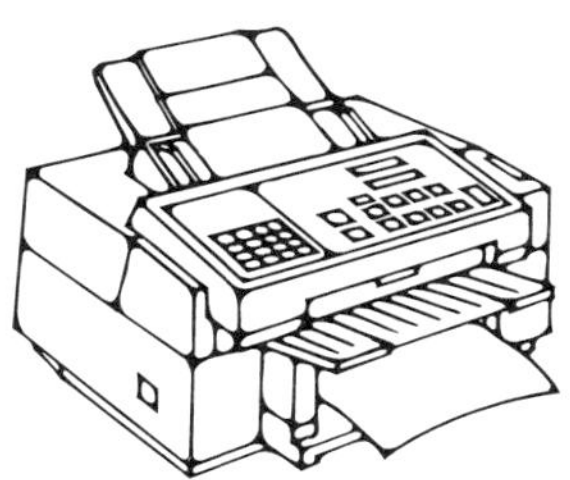

Uri's mother came home from work one day with a large box. She opened up the box and took out a strange looking machine. When Uri asked her what it was, she said it was a fax machine, something she used often for her job.

After his mother plugged the fax machine into the phone line and the electric outlet, they decided to try it out. Uri wanted to send a book report to his father who was still at work. Uri had gotten an "A" on the report. His mother turned the fax machine on, put the report in, and off went a copy to Uri's father.

A few minutes later, Uri heard the phone ring. He was surprised when the fax machine answered the phone. Uri was even more surprised when a note from his father came out of the machine. It said, "Good job, Uri. I'll be home in about half an hour."

5 Who came home first?

Ⓐ Uri

Ⓑ Uri's mother

Ⓒ Uri's father

6 What will the fax machine probably be used for?

Ⓕ For playing games and writing notes to Uri's friends

Ⓖ For work that Uri's mother must do at home

Ⓗ So Uri can write book reports and other school assignments

7 How does a fax send information from one place to another?

Ⓐ Through the television antenna

Ⓑ Through electric lines

Ⓒ Through telephone lines

8 What must Uri's father have at work?

Ⓕ A television

Ⓖ A fax machine

Ⓗ A computer

GO

Directions: Read or listen to the story. Choose the best answers to the questions about the story.

Warren Learns a Lesson

Warren wanted a puppy. He asked his mother and father every day to get him a puppy. They said a puppy was too much trouble. They didn't think Warren was big enough to take care of it. "We both work hard every day. You will have to feed him and take him out for a walk and brush him," they said. Warren said he could do that.

The family went to the animal shelter and picked out a nice, brown, furry puppy. Warren was so happy that he ran through the house chasing the puppy and laughing.

A few days later, Warren's mom had to wake him up early. She said, "Get up now. You must take the puppy out before you eat breakfast. Hurry."

One night, Warren had homework to do. His dad said, "Did you remember to feed the puppy?" Warren said he was too tired.

The puppy chewed things. It wasn't fun any more. "Take him back," Warren said. "A puppy is too much trouble to take care of."

His mom and dad would not let him give up the puppy. Warren had to care for him, even when he didn't want to.

After a while, the puppy grew up. Warren and his dog were best friends. Warren was happy because his family had kept the puppy.

9 Why did Warren's mom and dad make him take care of the puppy even when he didn't want to?

Ⓐ They were too tired to do it.

Ⓑ They wanted him to learn to do what he should.

Ⓒ They wanted to punish Warren.

Ⓓ They really did not like having the puppy in the house.

10 The puppy in the story was —

Ⓕ black.

Ⓖ white.

Ⓗ brown.

Ⓙ yellow.

11 The boxes show some things that happened in the story.

Warren wanted a puppy.	Warren got a puppy.		The puppy grew up.
1	2	3	4

Which of these belongs in box 3?

Ⓐ Warren's parents thought a puppy was too much trouble.

Ⓑ They took the puppy back to the animal shelter.

Ⓒ Warren did not want the puppy anymore.

Ⓓ Warren asked for a puppy every day.

GO

Directions: Read or listen to the story. Choose the best answers to the questions about the story.

Birdhouse

Making a birdhouse is fun and easy. Remember, though, you will need some help with cutting.

Use a large, empty, plastic, bleach bottle or other large, plastic bottle. Wash it out well. Punch two holes just below the lid. Tie a string through these holes. Leave a loop to hang the birdhouse.

Cut a hole near the bottom for the birds to enter. The hole should be about two inches wide. Different kinds of birds like holes of different sizes.

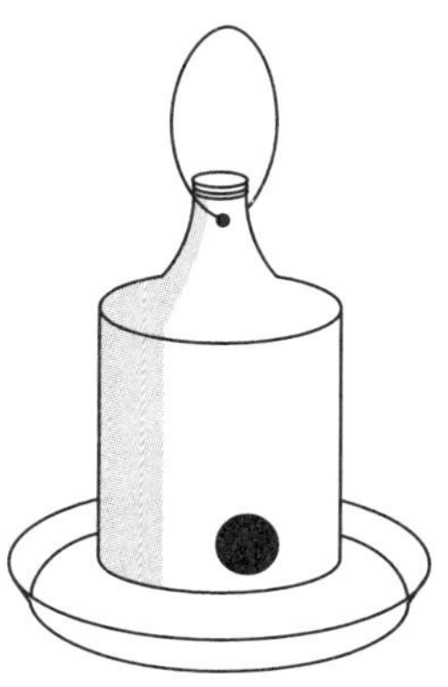

Glue a foil pie pan to the bottom of the bleach bottle. The birds can stand on this. Putting some seeds in the pan will attract birds to the house. When they see the opening, they will want to build a nest in it.

Hang your birdhouse in a nearby tree. Hang it high enough so cats will not be able to get to it.

12 To make a birdhouse from a bleach bottle, you must first—

Ⓕ hang it high in a tree.

Ⓖ punch two holes just under the lid.

Ⓗ put crumbs in the bottom.

Ⓙ wash it out well.

13 The foil pie pan glued to the bottom is for—

Ⓐ the birds to stand on.

Ⓑ hanging the birdhouse in the tree.

Ⓒ keeping cats out of the birdhouse.

Ⓓ the bird to build a nest.

14 What will make the birdhouse best for a small bird?

Ⓕ Washing it out

Ⓖ A small hole

Ⓗ Lots of seed

Ⓙ A large hole

15 Why would birds like a house like this one?

Ⓐ It would blow around if there was wind.

Ⓑ It would keep the rain off their nest.

Ⓒ It would be open on all sides.

Ⓓ The cats could get to it.

GO

Directions: Read or listen to the story. Choose the best answers to the questions about the story.

Did Nancy like her new school?

All the children in Nancy's town had to go to a different school for the third grade. Nancy was very afraid to go to a different school. She liked her old school and her teachers. She asked her mother if she could stay in second grade again.

"You must go with your class," her mother said. "Third grade will be lots of fun. You'll see."

Nancy thought she would not have to go to school if she pretended she was sick. She told her mother she was too sick to go to school. Nancy's mother knew that Nancy was really more afraid than she was sick. She took Nancy to school the first day. They walked into the new building together. She helped Nancy find her class.

Her new teacher was smiling and shook hands with Nancy's mother. The teacher said they were going to have a good third grade this year. Nancy saw Mary and Ellen and Tommy from her old class. By the time Nancy's mother left, she had forgotten about being afraid or sick. She was having a good time talking to her friends and meeting new ones. Third grade at a new school would be as much fun as last year had been.

16 Nancy was afraid of —

Ⓕ moving to a new town.

Ⓖ going to a new school.

Ⓗ losing all her old friends.

Ⓙ her new teacher.

17 Why did Nancy's mother go with her into the new classroom?

Ⓐ To see if there were any children there she knew

Ⓑ To tell the teacher that Nancy might feel sick

Ⓒ To help her feel better about the new school

Ⓓ To make sure she didn't run away

18 This story is about Nancy as she was beginning the —

Ⓕ first grade.

Ⓖ second grade.

Ⓗ third grade.

Ⓙ fourth grade.

19 When Nancy and her mother went into the classroom, the teacher was —

Ⓐ telling the children to sit down.

Ⓑ passing out books.

Ⓒ hanging up the children's coats.

Ⓓ smiling and welcoming the children.

Table of Contents
Language

Lesson 1 Listening Skills

Example **Directions:** Read or listen to the story. Then choose the best answer to the question.

A Joseph built a bird house. He used wood and nails. What object would he put it in to send it to his aunt? This one has been done for you.

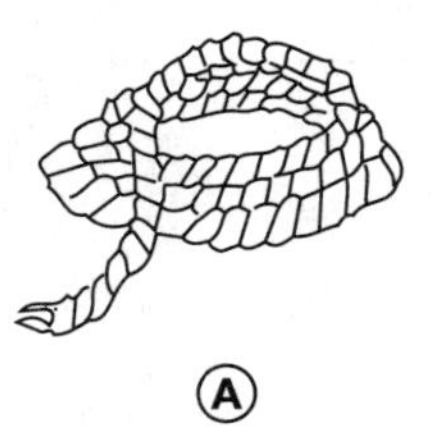

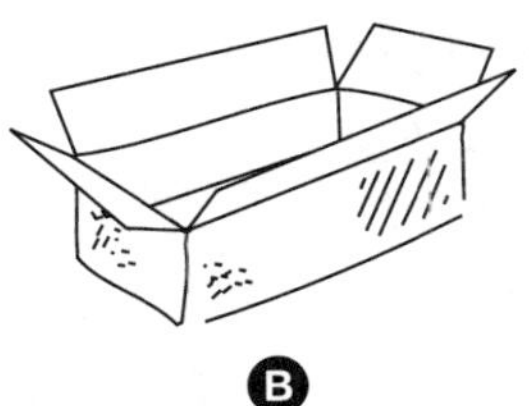

Ⓐ ● Ⓒ

Read or listen carefully to the story and look at all the pictures.

Do numbers 1-4 the same way.

Practice

1 Lettie likes sports. She tries a different sport during each season. Which sport does she do when it snows?

Ⓐ Ⓑ Ⓒ

2 Andrew wants a pet, but he lives in a small apartment. His parents said that he could have a small pet that could live in a bowl. Which pet did he choose?

Ⓕ Ⓖ Ⓗ

3 In the town of Lawnford, there is a place people enjoy. It has trees and grass. People like to sit under a tree on a summer day. Choose the picture that shows this place.

Ⓐ Ⓑ Ⓒ

4 Every night, Vera and her mother like to read a book together. Which picture shows what Vera and her mother like to do?

Ⓕ Ⓖ Ⓗ

STOP

Examples

A Estu likes to help her mom make dinner. When she helps her mom chop onions, her eyes water. What picture shows Estu after chopping onions?

Ⓐ

Ⓑ

Ⓒ

This one has been done for you. Do numbers 1-3 the same way.

B Look at these words. Which one is different from the other three? This one has been done for you. Do numbers 4-6 the same way.

Ⓕ shoe
Ⓖ hat
Ⓗ dish
Ⓙ pants

If you are not sure which answer is correct, take your best guess.

Practice

1 Petunia is a cat. She likes to sit in front of the fireplace to keep warm. Which picture shows Petunia keeping warm?

Ⓐ

Ⓑ

Ⓒ

2 Bob's favorite animal has a long neck and spots. Which is his favorite animal?

Ⓕ

Ⓖ

Ⓗ

3 Jonah wrote a story about something that is not real. What did he write a story about?

Ⓐ

Ⓑ

Ⓒ

4

Ⓕ car
Ⓖ truck
Ⓗ plane
Ⓙ move

5

Ⓐ and
Ⓑ house
Ⓒ but
Ⓓ or

6

Ⓕ rug
Ⓖ wall
Ⓗ floor
Ⓙ ceiling

E1 Directions: Listen to or read the story. Then choose the best answer to the question. Practice on this one. Do numbers 1-4 the same way.
Ms. McGill delivers mail in her neighborhood. Which one shows Ms. McGill?

Ⓐ

Ⓑ

Ⓒ

E2 Look at these words. Which one is different from the other three? This one has been done for you. Do numbers 5 and 6 the same way.

Ⓕ leaf
Ⓖ branch
● sand
Ⓙ root

1 Lynette needs to measure a piece of wood. What should she use?

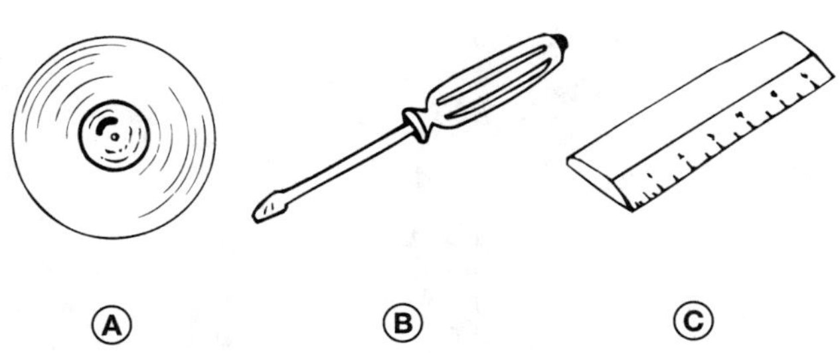
Ⓐ Ⓑ Ⓒ

2 At night, the cows on the farm go inside. The tractor goes in the barn. Where does the tractor go at night?

Ⓕ Ⓖ Ⓗ

3 Some parts of the United States are deserts. They are hot and dry and cactus plants grow there. Which one is a desert?

Ⓐ

Ⓑ

Ⓒ

5

Ⓐ orange
Ⓑ banana
Ⓒ apple
Ⓓ eat

4 Louis and his father like to go camping and fishing. Which picture shows what Louis and his father like to do?

Ⓕ

Ⓖ

Ⓗ

6

Ⓕ shoe
Ⓖ run
Ⓗ fly
Ⓙ swim

STOP

NUMBER RIGHT ______

Lesson 4 Capitalization

Examples **Directions:** This sentence is divided into three parts. Which part needs a capital letter? If the answer isn't shown, choose none.

This one has been done for you. Do numbers 1-3 the same way.

A	The store Ⓐ	on the corner Ⓑ	is closed. Ⓒ	None ●

Which part of the story needs another capital letter?

B Ⓕ The door is locked.

Ⓖ we can open it with

Ⓗ one of these keys.

Which word in the sentence should begin with a capital letter?

My friend lois won a prize.

C Ⓐ friend

Ⓑ lois

Ⓒ prize

Do numbers 4-6 the same way.

Sentences begin with capital letters.

Important words in a sentence begin with capital letters.

Practice

1	our teacher Ⓐ	likes to Ⓑ	go camping. Ⓒ	None Ⓓ
2	The coach of Ⓕ	the baseball team Ⓖ	is mr. Garcia. Ⓗ	None Ⓙ
3	I think that Ⓐ	this pizza is Ⓑ	too hot to eat. Ⓒ	None Ⓓ

STOP

4 Ⓕ The miller family moved

Ⓖ into a new house on

Ⓗ our street last week.

The fair opens on monday.

5 Ⓐ fair

Ⓑ open

Ⓒ monday

Look at the underlined part of the sentence. Which word should be capitalized?

The wind is blowing.

the sun is shining.
(1)

We should fly a kite.

6 Ⓕ the Sun

Ⓖ The sun

Ⓗ The phrase is capitalized correctly.

STOP

Lesson 5 Punctuation

Examples **Directions:** Is this sentence punctuated correctly? Choose the right punctuation mark. Choose None if no punctuation is needed.

This one has been done for you. Do numbers 1-3 the same way.

A Did you finish reading your book yet?

Ⓐ . Ⓑ ? Ⓒ ! ● None

Which part of the story needs another punctuation mark?

B Ⓕ A bird is in the tree

Ⓖ It has blue feathers

Ⓗ and sings a pretty song.

What punctuation mark should be added to the end of this sentence?

A large plane landed at the airport

C Ⓐ airport,

Ⓑ airport.

Ⓒ airport!

Look for missing punctuation at the end of the sentence.

Practice

1 How old are you

Ⓐ . Ⓑ ! Ⓒ ? Ⓓ None

2 This is my favorite soup.

Ⓕ ! Ⓖ , Ⓗ ? Ⓙ None

3 Jump out of the way

Ⓐ ? Ⓑ ! Ⓒ . Ⓓ None

STOP

Which sentence needs punctuation?

4 Ⓕ A painting of a lake

Ⓖ by M Caplan is hanging

Ⓗ in the office at our school.

Which phrase is punctuated correctly?

5 Ⓐ Dear Laura,

Ⓑ Dear Laura.

Ⓒ Dear Laura

Read or listen to the story. Look at the underlined part. Which punctuation does it need?

Is this your key
(1)
I found it near

your house today.

6 Ⓕ key!

Ⓖ key.

Ⓗ key?

Examples **Directions:** Look at each sentence. Which one is correct?

Practice on this one. Do numbers 1 and 2 the same way.

A Ⓐ we went shopping yesterday.

Ⓑ My mother and i bought clothes.

Ⓒ the stores were crowded.

Ⓓ These are my new shoes.

Look at the blank in each sentence. Choose the phrase that completes the sentence and is correctly punctuated and capitalized. Practice on this one. Do numbers 3-6 the same way.

Lara was born on **(B)** .

B Ⓕ june 2, 1990

Ⓖ June 2, 1990

Ⓗ June 2 1990

Ⓙ june 2 1990

Look for errors in capitalization. Then look for errors in punctuation.

Practice

1 Ⓐ Our game is on monday.

Ⓑ Jamie will stay over on friday.

Ⓒ Will you meet me on Wednesday afternoon?

Ⓓ What Day will you visit Nat?

2 Ⓕ That tree is very old.

Ⓖ How can you tell if this plant is healthy.

Ⓗ I planted flowers with Tim

Ⓙ Is that a rose bush

---

(3)

(4)

I miss all of you! Camp is fun, but I can't wait to come home.

(5)

Artie

3 Ⓐ March 4 1995

Ⓑ march 4, 1995

Ⓒ March 4, 1995

Ⓓ march 4 1995

4 Ⓕ Dear Mary,

Ⓖ dear mary

Ⓗ Dear mary,

Ⓙ dear Mary

5 Ⓐ Your Brother,

Ⓑ your brother

Ⓒ your brother,

Ⓓ Your brother,

GO

6

Moe Allen
4 King's Lane
____

Ⓕ Chicago Illinois 60656
Ⓖ chicago, illinois 60656
Ⓗ Chicago, Illinois 60656
Ⓙ Chicago, illinois 60656

Example **Directions:** Read the story. Look at the underlined part. Choose the answer that shows the correct capitalization and punctuation. Practice on this one.

C The rabbits heard a noise They ran away quickly.

Ⓐ noise. They
Ⓑ noise. they
Ⓒ noise? They
Ⓓ Best as it is

Do numbers 7-9 the same way.

(7) Our class had a picnic last week. We all met
(8) at the park on saturday morning. Everyone
(9) brought food to share. i brought fried chicken my
father made. The picnic was a lot of fun and we
want to do it again.

7
Ⓐ week we
Ⓑ Week. We
Ⓒ week, we
Ⓓ Best as it is

8
Ⓕ Saturday morning,
Ⓖ Saturday morning.
Ⓗ Saturday Morning.
Ⓙ Best as it is

9
Ⓐ share. I
Ⓑ share, I
Ⓒ share I.
Ⓓ Best as it is

STOP

Lesson 7 Test Yourself

Directions: Which part of the sentence needs a capital letter? Choose None if the sentence is correct as it is written. Do numbers 1-3 the same way.

E1 Do you think (A) | i can go (B) | with you tomorrow? (C) | None (D)

Which word or phrase needs a capital letter? Do numbers 4-7 the same way.

E2
(F) Mother says the rain
(G) will stop soon.
(H) then we can play.

E3 My brother will end his vacation on friday.
(A) brother
(B) vacation
(C) friday

1 The bowl on (A) | the table is (B) | very old. (C) | None (D)

2 will you (F) | go to the mall (G) | with your cousin? (H) | None (J)

3 Annie went to (A) | gymnastics class (B) | on wednesday. (C) | None (D)

STOP

4
(F) This book about science
(G) is very long, but i
(H) will finish it soon.

5
(A) Sam called dr. Brown
(B) to ask when she
(C) could visit our class.

6 I borrowed uncle Ben's basketball.
(F) uncle
(G) borrow
(H) basketball

7 My friend diane thought the movie was exciting.
(A) movie
(B) diane
(C) exciting

Let's sit outside.

It is a nice day. (1)

We can read or talk.

8
(F) nice Day
(G) Nice Day
(H) correct as it is written

STOP

Directions: Read or listen to the sentence. Is the sentence punctuated correctly? Choose the right answer. Practice on this one. Do numbers 10-11 the same way.

E4 Chet ran to the supermarket
Ⓕ . Ⓖ ? Ⓗ ! Ⓙ Correctly punctuated.

Which phrase needs punctuation? Do numbers 12 and 13 the same way.

E5 Ⓐ The tomatoes in
Ⓑ your garden are
Ⓒ growing very well

What punctuation mark should be added to the end of this sentence?
What time will you leave

E6 Ⓕ leave!
Ⓖ leave?
Ⓗ leave.

9 How did you know the answer?
Ⓐ . Ⓑ ! Ⓒ , Ⓓ None

10 Your shirt is in the closet
Ⓕ ! Ⓖ . Ⓗ ? Ⓙ None

11 Do you know where Bridget is
Ⓐ ? Ⓑ ! Ⓒ . Ⓓ None

STOP

12 Ⓕ The officer stopped the
Ⓖ cars The children crossed
Ⓗ the street carefully.

13 Ⓐ Ms Dawson is building
Ⓑ a table. She asked me
Ⓒ if I could help her.

How should the underlined phrase be punctuated and capitalized? Choose the best answer.

14 Dear Emily,
Thank you for the present.
<u>Your friend</u>
Katherine
Ⓕ Your friend.
Ⓖ Your friend
Ⓗ Your friend,

15 I cannot go.
Which one is a another word for cannot?
Ⓐ cant' Ⓑ can't Ⓒ ca'nt

Look at this letter. Look at the underlined part. Choose the right punctuation.

Thank you for the gloves.
They keep me warm.
<u>*Did you make them yourself*</u>
(1)

16 Ⓕ yourself?
Ⓖ yourself.
Ⓗ yourself!

STOP

Directions: Look at these sentences. Which one is capitalized correctly? This one has been done for you.

E7 Ⓐ delaware is a small state.

● Angela and her family visited Maine last summer.

Ⓒ Winter is cold in Iowa

Ⓓ Have you been to ohio?

Directions: Look at this sentence. Fill in the blank with the correctly capitalized name. This one has been done for you.

Tell ___(E8)___ that we are here.

E8 Ⓕ Mrs Burnham

Ⓖ Mrs. burnham

Ⓗ mrs. Burnham

● Mrs. Burnham

17 Ⓐ Emma bought this shirt in Dallas, Texas.

Ⓑ Tucson Arizona is hot and dry.

Ⓒ The traffic in Chicago illinois was very heavy.

Ⓓ Bret saw cowboys in butte, Montana.

18 Ⓕ The bus wont' be here for another ten minutes.

Ⓖ Wel'l all meet in front of the mall tomorrow.

Ⓗ Vanna doesn't want to go shopping.

Ⓙ Kevin ca'nt find the map.

Look at the blanks in this letter. Choose the words that fit in the blanks. Make sure your choice uses capitalization correctly.

> ___(19)___
>
> ___(20)___
>
> School will be finished soon. I would like to come and visit you at the lake.
>
> ___(21)___
>
> Annie

19 Ⓐ May 30, 1995

Ⓑ may 30 1995

Ⓒ May 30 1995

Ⓓ may 30, 1995

20 Ⓕ Dear Cindy

Ⓖ dear Cindy

Ⓗ Dear cindy

Ⓙ Dear Cindy,

21 Ⓐ Your Friend,

Ⓑ your friend

Ⓒ Your friend,

Ⓓ your Friend,

GO

22 Which choice should go in the blank? Make sure it is capitalized correctly.

Chris Chavez
224 Pueblo Street
____

Ⓕ Carson New Mexico 87761
Ⓖ carson, New Mexico 87761
Ⓗ carson New Mexico 87761
Ⓙ Carson, New Mexico 87761

E9 Let's visit Mr. Baker. He has not been feeling well.

Look at the sentences above. Look at the underlined part. Is it correct or should it be changed to one of the choices below?

Ⓐ Mr. baker
Ⓑ Mr Baker
Ⓒ mr. Baker
Ⓓ Correct

Look at the story. Look at the underlined part. Is it correct or should it be changed to one of the choices below?

(23) When ramona woke up she looked outside. It
(24) was snowing very hard. She quickly got dressed
and went downstairs. This was her first winter
(25) in idaho. She had never seen snow before.

23 Ⓐ Ramona Woke
Ⓑ Ramona woke
Ⓒ Ramona, woke
Ⓓ correct

24 Ⓕ hard she
Ⓖ Hard. She
Ⓗ hard She
Ⓙ correct

25 Ⓐ in Idaho.
Ⓑ in Idaho
Ⓒ In Idaho.
Ⓓ correct

Lesson 8 Usage

Examples **Directions:** Look at the sentence. What word should go in the blank or should substitute for the underlined part?

A This car is _______ than that one.	B This is <u>Omar's</u> friend.
Ⓐ fast ❸ faster Ⓒ fastest Ⓓ more faster This one has been done for you.	Ⓕ its Ⓖ him Ⓗ her Ⓙ his Practice on this one.

Stay with your first answer. It is usually right.

Practice

1 Both _______ are awake now.

Ⓐ puppy
Ⓑ puppies

2 The glass _______ when it fell from the table.

Ⓕ broke
Ⓖ break
Ⓗ breaked
Ⓙ breaking

3 A _______ bird flew by.

Ⓐ prettiest
Ⓑ more prettier
Ⓒ pretty
Ⓓ most prettiest

STOP

4 We found <u>the watch</u> under the tree in the park.

Ⓕ her
Ⓖ him
Ⓗ me
Ⓙ it

5 Did <u>your sister</u> call you yet?

Ⓐ her
Ⓑ them
Ⓒ she
Ⓓ they

STOP

Example Look at the sentences. Choose the one that is not correct. This one has been done for you.

C Ⓐ That is a nice bike.
● Me brother has one
Ⓒ just like it.

Do numbers 6-10 the same way.

6 Ⓕ Did you see the football
Ⓖ game on Sunday afternoon?
Ⓗ Julie and Randy was there.

7 Ⓐ No matter how hard we
Ⓑ try, we can't never catch
Ⓒ any fish in that lake.

8 Ⓕ Them there bananas
Ⓖ aren't ripe yet. Wait for
Ⓗ a day before eating them.

9 Ⓐ Is it time to go yet?
Ⓑ I and Ruth have been
Ⓒ ready for an hour.

10 Ⓕ Some ducks they have
Ⓖ been in the pond for
Ⓗ more than two weeks.

STOP

Look at the story. Look at the underlined part. Is it correct or should it be changed to one of the choices below?

The sky are blue today.
(1)
There are some pretty clouds.
The wind blows the clouds across the sky.
The clouds look like animals.
(2)
Animals that fly in the sky.

11 Ⓐ be
Ⓑ is
Ⓒ The way she did

12 Ⓕ looks
Ⓖ looking
Ⓗ The way she did

STOP

Examples

Directions: Look at the sentence. What word should fit in the blank? This one has been done for you. Do numbers 1-2 the same way.

A A truck _______ .

Ⓐ and a car

Ⓑ with big tires

Ⓒ around the corner

● is parked outside

Which one is a complete sentence? This one has been done for you. Do numbers 3-4 the same way.

B ● Lucinda had an apple after lunch.

Ⓖ An orange and a lemon.

Ⓗ Bananas from Mexico.

Ⓙ Raymond's favorite food watermelon.

A correct sentence contains a subject and a verb. It expresses a complete idea.

Practice

1 _______ marched in the parade.

Ⓐ Cold day

Ⓑ In the morning

Ⓒ Many people

Ⓓ Waving flags

2 A large box of toys _______ .

Ⓕ on the floor

Ⓖ was in the corner

Ⓗ for the children

Ⓙ will be buying

3 Ⓐ Running every day to practice for the race.

Ⓑ Beginning at Fourth and Main.

Ⓒ Many of my friends in the race.

Ⓓ The race will start at nine o'clock.

4 Ⓕ My mother works for a computer company.

Ⓖ Leaving the house early in the morning.

Ⓗ My father to school with me.

Ⓙ After school in the library.

STOP

Examples **Directions:** Which phrase is not part of a complete sentence?

This one has been done for you.	Practice on this one.
C Ⓐ A storm all night.	D Ⓕ Children playing there.
Ⓑ When we woke up	Ⓖ We live near a park.
Ⓒ it was still raining.	Ⓗ A cool place on a hot day.

Do numbers 5-8 the same way.

5 Ⓐ Martin and Paul helped
Ⓑ Mrs. Hogan mow the lawn.
Ⓒ Also raking up leaves.

6 Ⓕ Dinner at six o'clock.
Ⓖ Ellie did her homework
Ⓗ and then went to bed.

7 Ⓐ A letter in the mailbox.
Ⓑ Call Mollie or me tonight.
Ⓒ Looking for them.

8 Ⓕ To find some berries.
Ⓖ Having fun on a summer day.
Ⓗ Where did you go?

July 5, 1995

Dear Mom,
We had a picnic yesterday.
Uncle Mark and Aunt Linda made sandwiches.
To the lake drove we in the morning.
The water was very warm.

Love,
Sam

Look at this letter. Look at the underlined part. Is it clear as it is written or should it be changed to one of the choices below?

9 Ⓐ We drove to the lake in the morning.
Ⓑ In the morning we to the lake drove.
Ⓒ Clear as it is written.

Which sentence is clearly written?

10 Ⓕ Brenda and me they let go swimming.
Ⓖ They let Brenda and me go swimming.
Ⓗ To go swimming they let Brenda and me.

Example **Directions:** Which sentence fits in the blank in these paragraphs? This one has been done for you.

A Basketball is my favorite game. ________________________ . My friends like to play basketball, too.

Ⓐ Baseball is another game.

Ⓑ Playing sports is good exercise.

Ⓒ It is a nice day outside.

● I play basketball almost every day.

Do numbers 1 and 2 the same way.

A paragraph should focus on one idea. All the sentences in a paragraph should be related.

Practice

1 My friend Nancy has a pet fish. It lives in a bowl on a table. ________________________ .

Ⓐ Fish also live in the ocean and in lakes.

Ⓑ Nancy feeds her fish every day.

Ⓒ Nancy lives on my street.

Ⓓ My other friends live far away.

2 ________________________ . This is his first year in college. My brother wants to be a teacher.

Ⓕ My brother goes to college in Florida.

Ⓖ I have a brother and a sister.

Ⓗ Many people go to college.

Ⓙ My brother writes to me often.

Robert is going to write a letter to his grandmother about what he did over the weekend. What should he do before he writes his letter?

3 Ⓐ think about where his grandmother lives

Ⓑ write about his sister's favorite hobbies

Ⓒ write down what they did on the weekend

What should his letter be about?

4 Ⓕ what they did on the weekend

Ⓖ how to put shoes on

Ⓗ the mall where they bought shoes

May 12, 1995

Dear Grandmother,
Diana and I went to the mall yesterday.
We bought new shoes for the summer.
After we bought shoes we had lunch.
Diana has many friends at school.

Love,
Robert

Here is Robert's letter. Which sentence does not belong in this paragraph?

5 Ⓐ After we bought shoes we had lunch.

Ⓑ Diana has many friends at school.

Ⓒ Diana and I went to the mall yesterday.

Which sentence <u>does</u> belong in this paragraph?

6 Ⓕ There are different kinds of shoes.

Ⓖ Autumn comes after summer.

Ⓗ We ate pizza with mushrooms.

STOP

E1 Directions: Choose the word that fits in the blank. This one has been done for you.

How _______ is your dog?

- Ⓐ old (filled in)
- Ⓑ older
- Ⓒ oldest
- Ⓓ most old

E2 Directions: Choose the one that is a full sentence and is written correctly. This one has been done for you.

- Ⓕ Renting a video.
- Ⓖ Funny videos most of all.
- Ⓗ We all thought the video was very funny. (filled in)
- Ⓙ The store with many videos.

Do numbers 1-3 the same way.

1 How many _______ did you make?

- Ⓐ sandwich
- Ⓑ sandwiches

2 _______ walked from school to the playground.

- Ⓕ In the afternoon
- Ⓖ A group of children
- Ⓗ With the teacher
- Ⓙ Sun is shining

3 Please hand <u>Cassie</u> the box of crayons.

- Ⓐ her
- Ⓑ it
- Ⓒ she
- Ⓓ them

Do numbers 4-6 the same way.

4
- Ⓕ It was a nicest day for a hike to the lake.
- Ⓖ Catherine woke up earlier today than she did yesterday.
- Ⓗ The bike's tire was most flattest.
- Ⓙ Dana caught a tiniest fish.

5
- Ⓐ The workers made the door to our apartment wider.
- Ⓑ My grandmother come to live with us.
- Ⓒ My parents wants to make her feel welcome.
- Ⓓ Her room are next to mine.

6
- Ⓕ Wood from my back yard.
- Ⓖ Working carefully so not to get hurt.
- Ⓗ Mother helping us.
- Ⓙ Let's build a tree house.

E3 Read or listen to the story. Mark the circle in front of the part of the story that has a mistake. This one has been done for you. Do numbers 7 and 8 the same way.

- Ⓐ (filled) We rode to the river.
- Ⓑ The boats were racing, and
- Ⓒ we wanted to watch.

E4 Fill in the circle in front of the answer choice that is a complete sentence. Do numbers 9 and 10 the same way.

- Ⓕ Pillows on the floor.
- Ⓖ Where is the game?
- Ⓗ Sitting near the window.

7
- Ⓐ Buddy wanted to help
- Ⓑ his mother cook dinner.
- Ⓒ Washing the vegetables.

8
- Ⓕ Stacey told Fred that
- Ⓖ this was the bigger box
- Ⓗ she could find in the closet.

9
- Ⓐ The stamps are on the desk.
- Ⓑ Writing a story about pets.
- Ⓒ Paper folded in half.

10
- Ⓕ Turning the lamp off.
- Ⓖ Near the kitchen window.
- Ⓗ The flowers are on the table.

STOP

My friend Alan call me yesterday.
(1)
He wanted me to go to his house.
I asked my mother if I could.
She said I could.
Alan and I with his computer played.
We also wrote some letters.

Look at these sentences. Look at the first underlined part. Is it correct or should it be changed to one of the choices below?

11
- Ⓐ calling
- Ⓑ called
- Ⓒ Correct as it is written

Look at the second underlined part. Is it correct as it is written or should it be changed to one of the choices below?

12
- Ⓕ Alan and I played with his computer.
- Ⓖ With his computer played Alan and I.
- Ⓗ Correct as it is written

Directions: Look at this paragraph. Which sentence should go in the blank?

This one has been done for you.

E5 Devon lives in a big apartment building. ______________________ . She can take the elevator, but she likes to walk up the stairs.

- Ⓐ Cities have many tall buildings.
- ● Her apartment is on the tenth floor.
- Ⓒ Jorge lives on a street with many trees.
- Ⓓ She walks to school with her friends.

Do numbers 13 and 14 the same way.

13 On Sunday we went for a ride in the country. We saw many farms with horses and cows. ______________________ .

- Ⓐ On Monday I will go back to school.
- Ⓑ Milk comes from cows on a farm.
- Ⓒ There are more things to do in the city.
- Ⓓ On the way home we saw some deer.

14 ______________________ . She wants to buy a present for her mother. Her mother's birthday is in October.

- Ⓕ Julie is saving her money.
- Ⓖ Julie's mother is a doctor.
- Ⓗ Many people have a party on their birthday.
- Ⓙ Buying a birthday present is fun.

STOP

Look at this paragraph. Which sentence would be a good topic sentence?

He uses the truck for his job.

My cousin is a farmer.

He will carry many things in the truck.

15
- Ⓐ I have an uncle named Harvey.
- Ⓑ My uncle bought a new truck.
- Ⓒ Farmers work very hard.

STOP

NUMBER RIGHT ______

Lesson 12 Spelling Skills

Directions: Which word fits in the sentence and is spelled correctly?

A I didn't ________ the window.	**B** Do you want a ________ of milk?
Ⓐ breack Ⓒ bracke	Ⓕ glas Ⓗ glasc
● break Ⓓ brayk	Ⓖ galass Ⓙ glass
This one has been done for you.	Practice on this one.

If an item is too difficult, skip it and move on to another one. Come back later to the item you skipped.

Do numbers 1-6 the same way.

Practice

1 Be careful you don't ________ .

Ⓐ fall　Ⓒ fal

Ⓑ fawll　Ⓓ fawl

2 Regina is the ________ on our baseball team.

Ⓕ pitchr　Ⓗ pitcher

Ⓖ petcher　Ⓙ picher

3 A cat can ________ very high.

Ⓐ leap　Ⓒ lepe

Ⓑ leep　Ⓓ liep

4 When will you ________ ?

Ⓕ retern　Ⓗ retirn

Ⓖ return　Ⓙ riturn

5 Shakeen will ________ for us.

Ⓐ seng　Ⓒ sinng

Ⓑ singk　Ⓓ sing

6 A ________ is sitting on our lawn.

Ⓕ rabit　Ⓗ rabitt

Ⓖ rabbit　Ⓙ rebbit

STOP

Examples

Directions: Choose the word that is <u>not</u> spelled correctly.

This one has been done for you.	Practice on this one.
C jump Ⓐ over Ⓑ shair ●	**D** Ⓕ knee Ⓖ poor Ⓗ derty Ⓙ feel

Do numbers 7-14 the same way.

7

farmer Ⓐ   darive Ⓑ   fair Ⓒ

8

large Ⓕ   family Ⓖ   kitchn Ⓗ

9

anie Ⓐ   paint Ⓑ   ground Ⓒ

10

watch Ⓕ   fish Ⓖ   whater Ⓗ

11 Ⓐ barck
Ⓑ yell
Ⓒ hot
Ⓓ smooth

12 Ⓕ all
Ⓖ cover
Ⓗ tharow
Ⓙ ring

13 Ⓐ sleep
Ⓑ inside
Ⓒ brick
Ⓓ docter

14 Ⓕ bend
Ⓖ sherp
Ⓗ drop
Ⓙ wonder

STOP

Directions: Look at this sentence. Look at the underlined words. Which one is spelled incorrectly?

E Flowers grew biside the road. Ⓐ ● Ⓒ	This one has been done for you.

Do numbers 15-20 the same way.

15 Tony will visit his grandmother next munth.

Ⓐ Ⓑ Ⓒ

16 Did you lock the doar before you left?

Ⓕ Ⓖ Ⓗ

17 Phoebe felt sik this morning.

Ⓐ Ⓑ Ⓒ

18 A bear walkt slowly into the woods.

Ⓕ Ⓖ Ⓗ

19 The lamp on the table is brocken.

Ⓐ Ⓑ Ⓒ

20 We had a falat tire on the way to school.

Ⓕ Ⓖ Ⓗ

STOP

Directions: Which word is spelled correctly and fits in the sentence?

E1 Who sits ________ you? Ⓐ bihind ● behind Ⓑ beheind Ⓓ behinde This one has been done for you.	Practice one this one. **E2** Stephanie dropped her ________ . Ⓕ shoe Ⓗ showe Ⓖ sho Ⓙ shou

Do numbers 1-10 the same way.

1 It is too ________ to keep playing.

Ⓐ dirk Ⓒ darck
Ⓑ derk Ⓓ dark

2 That was the ________ banana.

Ⓕ lasd Ⓗ laste
Ⓖ last Ⓙ lastt

3 We will ________ tomorrow.

Ⓐ practice Ⓒ practis
Ⓑ practise Ⓓ prectice

4 Barbara will ________ us.

Ⓕ folow Ⓗ follow
Ⓖ follo Ⓙ folloe

5 Vince tore his ________ while he was climbing the tree.

Ⓐ shirt Ⓒ chirt
Ⓑ shert Ⓓ schirt

6 This is a ________ story.

Ⓕ troo Ⓗ trou
Ⓖ tru Ⓙ true

7 The river is ________ here.

Ⓐ weid Ⓒ wyde
Ⓑ wide Ⓓ whyde

8 That is a ________ flashlight.

Ⓕ bright Ⓗ brigt
Ⓖ brite Ⓙ brait

9 ________ the street carefully.

Ⓐ Cros Ⓒ Craws
Ⓑ Kross Ⓓ Cross

10 They will have to ________ to get home on time.

Ⓕ rushe Ⓗ ruch
Ⓖ rush Ⓙ rusch

STOP

Directions: Which word is spelled incorrectly?

E3 This one has been done for you.	**E4** Practice on this one.
whair (A, filled) · old (B) · clock (C)	(F) pear (G) hit (H) ackt (J) land

Do numbers 11-18 the same way.

11

hand (A) · still (B) · hert (C)

12

offise (F) · busy (G) · place (H)

13

funny (A) · monkie (B) · played (C)

14

glad (F) · visit (G) · parck (H)

15
- (A) light
- (B) get
- (C) nock
- (D) shame

16
- (F) raize
- (G) ear
- (H) never
- (J) boot

17
- (A) hill
- (B) stone
- (C) cary
- (D) cost

18
- (F) chicken
- (G) rede
- (H) bite
- (J) search

STOP

Directions: Look at the underlined words in each sentence. Which one is spelled incorrectly?

E5 Our school is near the lacke.

Ⓐ school Ⓑ near ● lacke

This one has been done for you.

Do numbers 19-25 the same way.

19 Did you viset your uncle last week?

Ⓐ viset Ⓑ uncle Ⓒ week

20 We saw a turtel in the garden.

Ⓕ saw Ⓖ turtel Ⓗ garden

21 Can you help me clene up my room?

Ⓐ help Ⓑ clene Ⓒ room

22 Hattie says she can hear the train from her hous.

Ⓕ hear Ⓖ train Ⓗ hous

23 Ron's grandmother tryes to walk a mile every day after lunch.

Ⓐ tryes Ⓑ every Ⓒ lunch

24 The buket is on the shelf in the garage.

Ⓕ buket Ⓖ shelf Ⓗ garage

25 My shoes are almost woren out.

Ⓐ shoes Ⓑ almost Ⓒ woren

STOP

NUMBER RIGHT ______

Lesson 14 Study Skills

Example **Directions:** This table of contents is from a book about transportation. Use it to answer the question.

If you look on page 14, will you find information about transportation in the sky, in water, or on the ground?

Table of Contents

A Ⓐ sky

Ⓑ water

Ⓒ ground

This one has been done for you.

Think about the question and look at all the choices before you choose an answer.

Practice Look at this table of contents. It is from a book about Canada.

Table of Contents

What page would you look on to find information about mountains in Canada?

1 Ⓐ 19

Ⓑ 32

Ⓒ 44

What would you find on page 50?

2 Ⓕ who discovered Canada

Ⓖ names of Canadian cities

Ⓗ how Canadians have fun

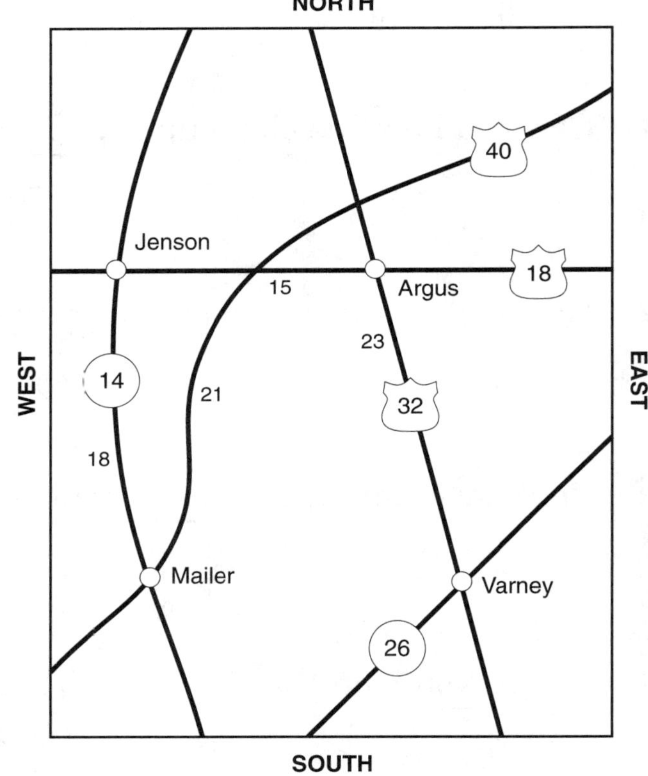

Look at this map.

3 What town is located where Highway 32 crosses Highway 18?

Ⓐ Mailer

Ⓑ Argus

Ⓒ Varney

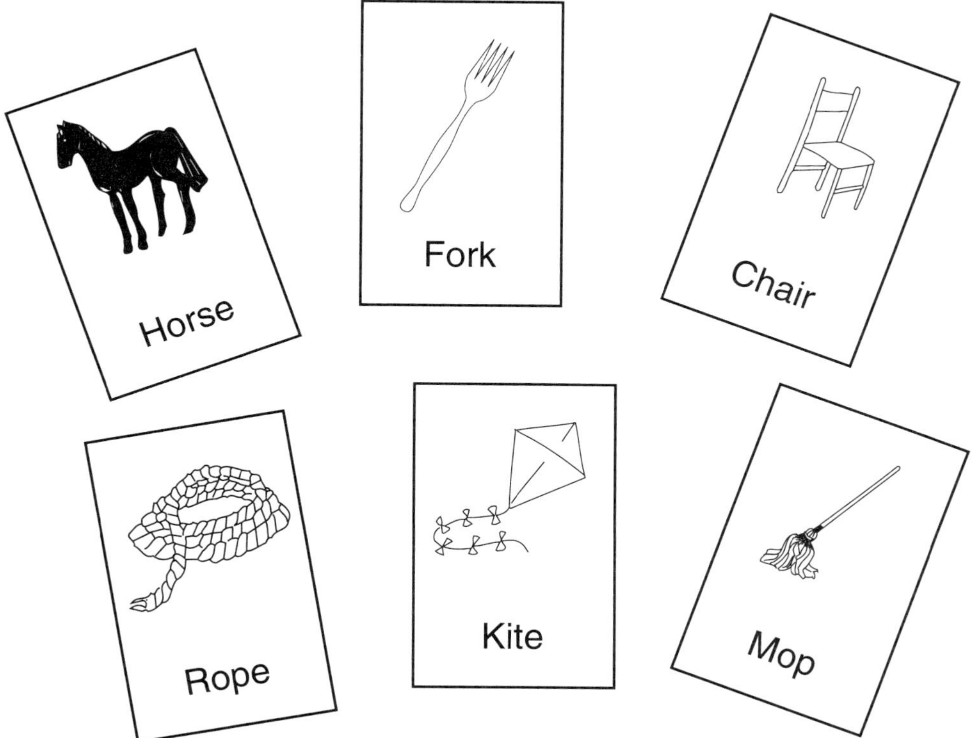

Look at these cards. Think about how you would arrange them in alphabetical order. Then answer these questions.

4 Which picture should be at the very top of the page?

Ⓕ Horse

Ⓖ Kite

Ⓗ Chair

5 Which picture should be the fourth one on the page?

Ⓐ Kite

Ⓑ Horse

Ⓒ Rope

6 Which picture should be between the kite and the rope?

Ⓕ Mop

Ⓖ Horse

Ⓗ Fork

7 Which picture should be the last one on the page?

Ⓐ Mop

Ⓑ Rope

Ⓒ Kite

STOP

Directions: Look at these definitions. Then answer the questions.

achieve
To do very well at something

E1 How do you spell a word that means "to do very well"?

Ⓐ acheive

Ⓑ atchieve

● achieve

This one has been done for you.

antique
From an earlier time

anvil
A large iron object used for hammering

conduct
To lead a group of musicians

gallop
To run quickly with large steps

gear
A toothed wheel used in machines

leap
To jump into the air

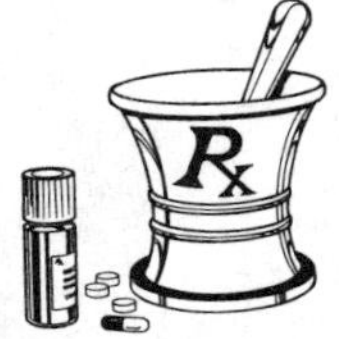

prescription
Medicine that has been ordered by a doctor

Do numbers 1-3 the same way.

1 What might you be given if you are sick?

Ⓐ leap

Ⓑ anvil

Ⓒ prescription

2 Which word fits best in the sentence "This ________ table is over a hundred years old."

Ⓕ antique

Ⓖ gear

Ⓗ anvil

3 How do you spell the name of part of a machine?

Ⓐ leap

Ⓑ gear

Ⓒ conduct

STOP

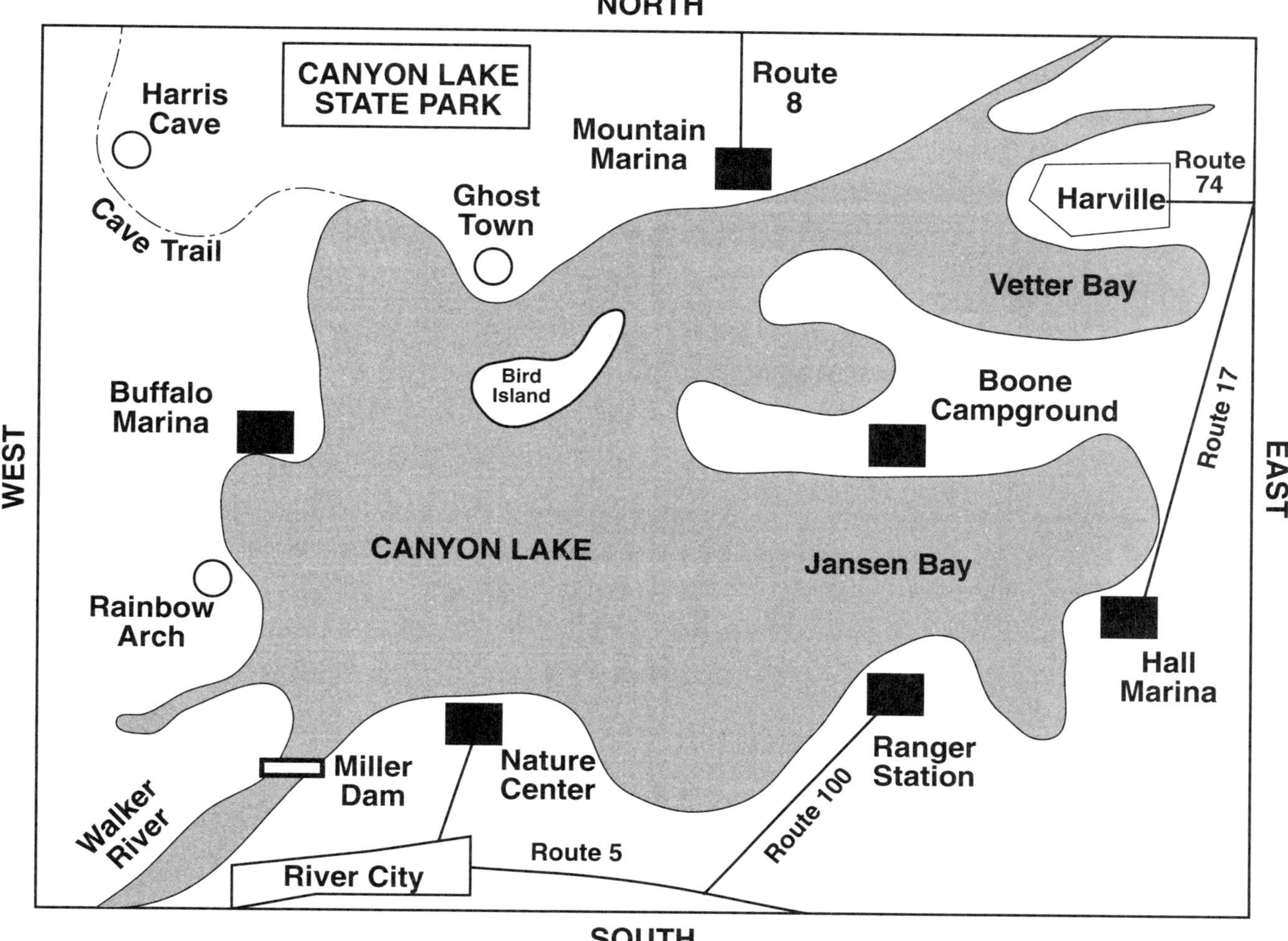

Directions: Look at the map. Then answer the questions.

4 Which is closest to Miller Dam?

Ⓕ Nature Center

Ⓖ Mountain Marina

Ⓗ Ghost Town

5 Which is north of the Ranger Station?

Ⓐ Nature Center

Ⓑ Boone Campground

Ⓒ River City

6 Which road leads to Harville?

Ⓕ Route 8

Ⓖ Route 5

Ⓗ Route 74

7 Which direction is Buffalo Marina from Bird Island?

Ⓐ North

Ⓑ West

Ⓒ East

STOP

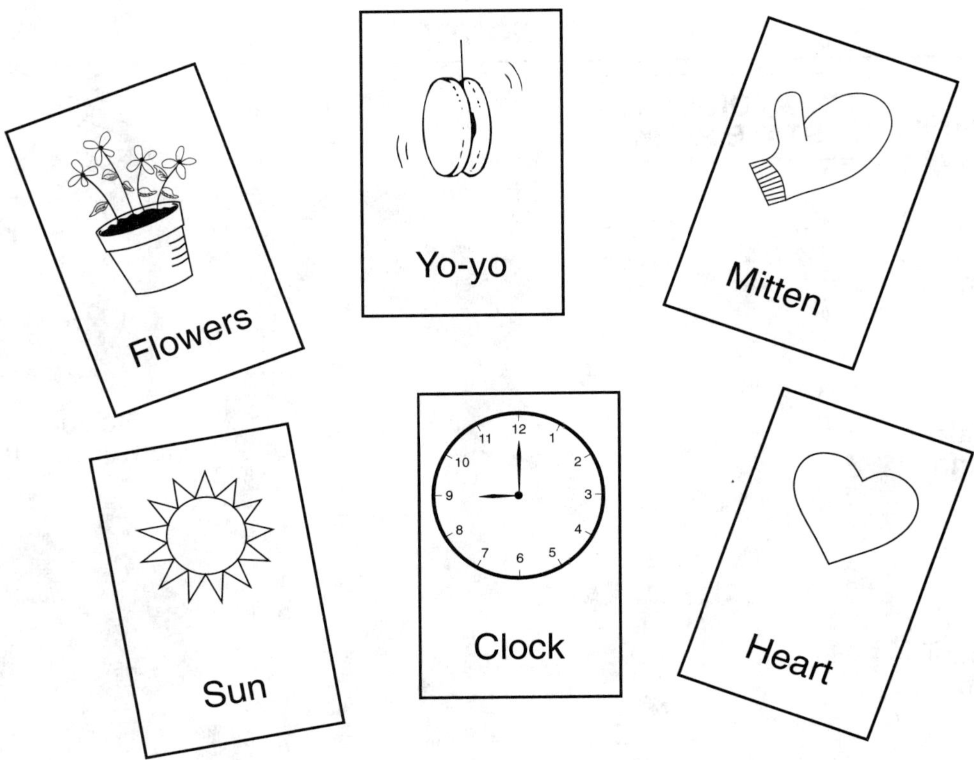

Directions: Look at these cards. Think about how you would arrange them in alphabetical order. Then answer these questions.

8 Which picture should be at the very top of the page?

Ⓕ Flowers

Ⓖ Clock

Ⓗ Mitten

9 Which picture should come right after the heart?

Ⓐ Yo-yo

Ⓑ Flowers

Ⓒ Mitten

10 Which picture should be between the mitten and the yo-yo?

Ⓕ Flowers

Ⓖ Heart

Ⓗ Sun

11 Which picture should be the last one on the page?

Ⓐ Yo-yo

Ⓑ Sun

Ⓒ Heart

STOP

NUMBER RIGHT ______

Name and Answer Sheet

To the Student:

These tests will give you a chance to put the tips you have learned to work.

A few last reminders . . .

- Be sure you understand all the directions before you begin each test. You may ask the teacher questions about the directions if you do not understand them.
- Work as quickly as you can during each test.
- When you change an answer, be sure to erase your first mark completely.
- You can guess at an answer or skip difficult items and go back to them later.
- Use the tips you have learned whenever you can.
- It is OK to be a little nervous. You may even do better.

Now that you have completed the lessons in this unit, you are on your way to scoring high!

STUDENT'S NAME

LAST | FIRST | MI

(Each of the 11 LAST columns, 6 FIRST columns and 1 MI column: ○ Ⓐ Ⓑ Ⓒ Ⓓ Ⓔ Ⓕ Ⓖ Ⓗ Ⓘ Ⓙ Ⓚ Ⓛ Ⓜ Ⓝ Ⓞ Ⓟ Ⓠ Ⓡ Ⓢ Ⓣ Ⓤ Ⓥ Ⓦ Ⓧ Ⓨ Ⓩ)

SCHOOL

TEACHER

FEMALE ○ MALE ○

BIRTH DATE

MONTH	DAY		YEAR	
JAN ○	0	0		0
FEB ○	1	1		1
MAR ○	2	2		2
APR ○	3	3		3
MAY ○		4		4
JUN ○		5	5	5
JUL ○		6	6	6
AUG ○		7	7	7
SEP ○		8	8	8
OCT ○		9	9	9
NOV ○				
DEC ○				

GRADE

① ② ③

PART 1 LISTENING

E1 Ⓐ Ⓑ Ⓒ Ⓓ
E2 Ⓕ Ⓖ Ⓗ Ⓙ
1 Ⓐ Ⓑ Ⓒ Ⓓ
2 Ⓕ Ⓖ Ⓗ Ⓙ
3 Ⓐ Ⓑ Ⓒ Ⓓ
4 Ⓕ Ⓖ Ⓗ Ⓙ
5 Ⓐ Ⓑ Ⓒ Ⓓ
6 Ⓕ Ⓖ Ⓗ Ⓙ

PART 2 LANGUAGE MECHANICS

E1 Ⓐ Ⓑ Ⓒ Ⓓ
E2 Ⓕ Ⓖ Ⓗ Ⓙ
E3 Ⓐ Ⓑ Ⓒ Ⓓ
E4 Ⓕ Ⓖ Ⓗ Ⓙ
E5 Ⓐ Ⓑ Ⓒ Ⓓ
E6 Ⓕ Ⓖ Ⓗ Ⓙ
E7 Ⓐ Ⓑ Ⓒ Ⓓ
E8 Ⓕ Ⓖ Ⓗ Ⓙ
E9 Ⓐ Ⓑ Ⓒ Ⓓ
1 Ⓐ Ⓑ Ⓒ Ⓓ
2 Ⓕ Ⓖ Ⓗ Ⓙ
3 Ⓐ Ⓑ Ⓒ Ⓓ
4 Ⓕ Ⓖ Ⓗ Ⓙ
7 Ⓐ Ⓑ Ⓒ Ⓓ
8 Ⓕ Ⓖ Ⓗ Ⓙ
9 Ⓐ Ⓑ Ⓒ Ⓓ
10 Ⓕ Ⓖ Ⓗ Ⓙ
11 Ⓐ Ⓑ Ⓒ Ⓓ
12 Ⓕ Ⓖ Ⓗ Ⓙ
13 Ⓐ Ⓑ Ⓒ Ⓓ
14 Ⓕ Ⓖ Ⓗ Ⓙ
15 Ⓐ Ⓑ Ⓒ Ⓓ
16 Ⓕ Ⓖ Ⓗ Ⓙ
17 Ⓐ Ⓑ Ⓒ Ⓓ
18 Ⓕ Ⓖ Ⓗ Ⓙ
19 Ⓐ Ⓑ Ⓒ Ⓓ
20 Ⓕ Ⓖ Ⓗ Ⓙ
21 Ⓐ Ⓑ Ⓒ Ⓓ
22 Ⓕ Ⓖ Ⓗ Ⓙ
23 Ⓐ Ⓑ Ⓒ Ⓓ
24 Ⓕ Ⓖ Ⓗ Ⓙ
25 Ⓐ Ⓑ Ⓒ Ⓓ

PART 3 LANGUAGE EXPRESSION

E1 Ⓐ Ⓑ Ⓒ Ⓓ
E2 Ⓕ Ⓖ Ⓗ Ⓙ
E3 Ⓐ Ⓑ Ⓒ Ⓓ
E4 Ⓕ Ⓖ Ⓗ Ⓙ
E5 Ⓐ Ⓑ Ⓒ Ⓓ
1 Ⓐ Ⓑ Ⓒ Ⓓ
2 Ⓕ Ⓖ Ⓗ Ⓙ
3 Ⓐ Ⓑ Ⓒ Ⓓ
4 Ⓕ Ⓖ Ⓗ Ⓙ
5 Ⓐ Ⓑ Ⓒ Ⓓ
6 Ⓕ Ⓖ Ⓗ Ⓙ
7 Ⓐ Ⓑ Ⓒ Ⓓ
8 Ⓕ Ⓖ Ⓗ Ⓙ
9 Ⓐ Ⓑ Ⓒ Ⓓ
10 Ⓕ Ⓖ Ⓗ Ⓙ
11 Ⓐ Ⓑ Ⓒ Ⓓ
12 Ⓕ Ⓖ Ⓗ Ⓙ
13 Ⓐ Ⓑ Ⓒ Ⓓ
14 Ⓕ Ⓖ Ⓗ Ⓙ
15 Ⓐ Ⓑ Ⓒ Ⓓ
16 Ⓕ Ⓖ Ⓗ Ⓙ
17 Ⓐ Ⓑ Ⓒ Ⓓ
18 Ⓕ Ⓖ Ⓗ Ⓙ

PART 4 SPELLING

E1 Ⓐ Ⓑ Ⓒ Ⓓ
E2 Ⓕ Ⓖ Ⓗ Ⓙ
E3 Ⓐ Ⓑ Ⓒ Ⓓ
E4 Ⓕ Ⓖ Ⓗ Ⓙ
E5 Ⓐ Ⓑ Ⓒ Ⓓ
1 Ⓐ Ⓑ Ⓒ Ⓓ
2 Ⓕ Ⓖ Ⓗ Ⓙ
3 Ⓐ Ⓑ Ⓒ Ⓓ
4 Ⓕ Ⓖ Ⓗ Ⓙ
5 Ⓐ Ⓑ Ⓒ Ⓓ
6 Ⓕ Ⓖ Ⓗ Ⓙ
7 Ⓐ Ⓑ Ⓒ Ⓓ
8 Ⓕ Ⓖ Ⓗ Ⓙ
9 Ⓐ Ⓑ Ⓒ Ⓓ
10 Ⓕ Ⓖ Ⓗ Ⓙ
11 Ⓐ Ⓑ Ⓒ Ⓓ
12 Ⓕ Ⓖ Ⓗ Ⓙ
13 Ⓐ Ⓑ Ⓒ Ⓓ
14 Ⓕ Ⓖ Ⓗ Ⓙ
15 Ⓐ Ⓑ Ⓒ Ⓓ
16 Ⓕ Ⓖ Ⓗ Ⓙ
17 Ⓐ Ⓑ Ⓒ Ⓓ
18 Ⓕ Ⓖ Ⓗ Ⓙ
19 Ⓐ Ⓑ Ⓒ Ⓓ
20 Ⓕ Ⓖ Ⓗ Ⓙ
21 Ⓐ Ⓑ Ⓒ Ⓓ
22 Ⓕ Ⓖ Ⓗ Ⓙ
23 Ⓐ Ⓑ Ⓒ Ⓓ
24 Ⓕ Ⓖ Ⓗ Ⓙ
25 Ⓐ Ⓑ Ⓒ Ⓓ

PART 5 STUDY SKILLS

E1 Ⓐ Ⓑ Ⓒ Ⓓ
1 Ⓐ Ⓑ Ⓒ Ⓓ
2 Ⓕ Ⓖ Ⓗ Ⓙ
3 Ⓐ Ⓑ Ⓒ Ⓓ
4 Ⓕ Ⓖ Ⓗ Ⓙ
5 Ⓐ Ⓑ Ⓒ Ⓓ
6 Ⓕ Ⓖ Ⓗ Ⓙ
7 Ⓐ Ⓑ Ⓒ Ⓓ
8 Ⓕ Ⓖ Ⓗ Ⓙ

STOP

Part 1 Listening

E1 Directions: Read or listen to the sentences. Then choose the best answer to the question.

Cows lie down when they are tired.
Which picture shows what a cow does when it is tired?

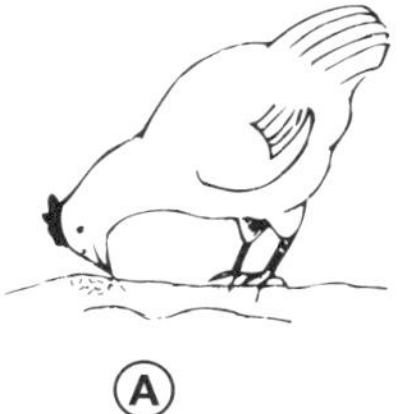
Ⓐ

● B

Ⓒ

This one has been done for you.
Do numbers 1-4 the same way.

E2 Directions: Look at these words. Which one is different from the other three? This one has been done for you.

Ⓕ sofa
Ⓖ chair
Ⓗ bench
● J sit

Do numbers 5 and 6 the same way.

1 Gilda learned to fly through the air. Which picture shows Gilda?

Ⓐ Ⓑ Ⓒ

2 Kurt is going on a vacation to a ranch. He already has cowboy boots and a shirt. Which picture shows what else Kurt will need?

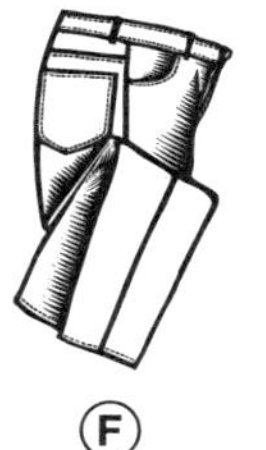
Ⓕ

Ⓖ

Ⓗ

3 Della's cat was tired. It fell asleep on something made of wood. Which picture shows where Della's cat slept?

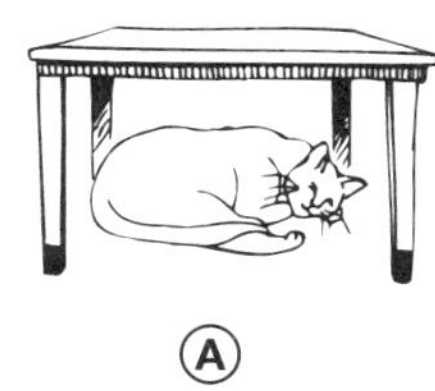
Ⓐ

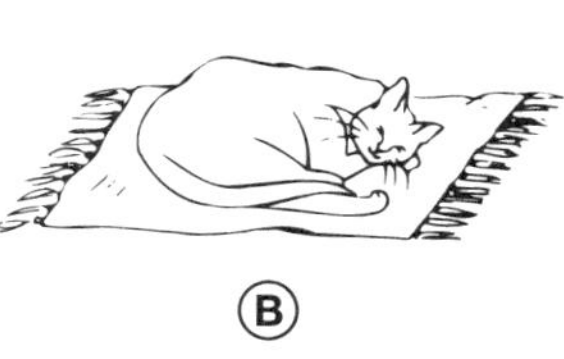
Ⓑ

Ⓒ

4 Marnie went for a ride in a boat. She caught something that swims in the lake. Which picture shows Marnie and what she caught?

Ⓕ

Ⓖ

Ⓗ

5

Ⓐ winter
Ⓑ season
Ⓒ fall
Ⓓ spring

6

Ⓕ sun
Ⓖ moon
Ⓗ night
Ⓙ stars

STOP

Part 2 Language Mechanics

Directions: Which part of each sentence has a mistake? If there is no mistake, choose None.

This one has been done for you.

E1 the package (A) | is too large (B) | for me to carry. (C) | None (D)

Do this one the same way.

E2 Ⓕ The basket of fruit

Ⓖ is a gift from my sister's

Ⓗ best friend, kim.

Do numbers 1–5 the same way.

Which word in the sentence should begin with a capital letter?

The soccer game will be on tuesday at noon.

E3 Ⓐ game Ⓑ tuesday Ⓒ noon

Do numbers 6 and 7 the same way.

1 Our teacher Ⓐ | told marty that Ⓑ | he sings well. Ⓒ | None Ⓓ

2 the monkeys Ⓕ | at the zoo Ⓖ | were very funny. Ⓗ | None Ⓙ

3 We played Ⓐ | baseball at the park Ⓑ | until it got dark. Ⓒ | None Ⓓ

STOP

4 Ⓕ Please call Aunt Vicki.

Ⓖ she will be home between

Ⓗ three and four o'clock.

5 Ⓐ The trees in the

Ⓑ park were planted last

Ⓒ year by mr. Williamson.

Choose the word that should begin with a capital letter.

most of my friends can swim.

6 Ⓕ most

Ⓖ friends

Ⓗ swim

My sister was born in april.

7 Ⓐ sister

Ⓑ born

Ⓒ april

My dog's name is Rachel.

She comes when i call her. (1) [underlined: i call]

She likes to chew on bones.

Look at the sentences. Look at the underlined part. Choose the correct way that part should be written.

8 Ⓕ I call

Ⓖ I Call

Ⓗ i Call

STOP

Directions: Choose the best answer to each question. These have been done for you.

Look at this sentence. Is it punctuated correctly? Choose the correct punctuation. Choose None if no punctuation is needed.

E4 This is the largest room in the house.
Ⓕ . Ⓖ ? Ⓗ ! Ⓙ None

Which of these choices needs a punctuation mark?

E5 Ⓐ Aunt Jane helped us
● bake bread We served
Ⓒ it to our friends at dinner.

Which choice shows the correct punctuation for the sentence?

Where is the fire

E6 Ⓕ fire.
● fire?
Ⓗ fire!

Choose the correct punctuation for the sentence. Choose None if no punctuation is needed.

9 Let's walk down to the river and watch the boats
Ⓐ , Ⓑ ! Ⓒ . Ⓓ None

10 Where is the nearest post office
Ⓕ ! Ⓖ . Ⓗ ? Ⓙ None

11 Did you remember to turn the water off?
Ⓐ ? Ⓑ ! Ⓒ . Ⓓ None

STOP

Which of these choices needs a punctuation mark?

12 Ⓕ This note is from
Ⓖ B Allen. She stayed
Ⓗ with us last week.

13 Ⓐ We were having
Ⓑ such a good time we
Ⓒ forgot to check the time

Which choice shows the correct punctuation for the sentence?

14 This isnt my coat.
Ⓕ isn't
Ⓖ isnt'
Ⓗ is'nt

15 How tall are you
Ⓐ you.
Ⓑ you!
Ⓒ you?

Peggy is my new friend
(1)
She goes to my school.
I like to play tennis with Peggy.

Look at these sentences. Look at the underlined part. Which choice shows the correct punctuation for that part?

16 Ⓕ friend.
Ⓖ friend?
Ⓗ friend!

Directions: Which sentence is written correctly?

E7 Ⓐ what can we do today?

Ⓑ We can meet cindy at the park.

● This is Bob's basketball.

Ⓓ The basketball court is on second avenue.

This one has been done for you.
Do numbers 17 and 18 the same way.

Directions: Choose the phrase that fits in the blank and has correct capitalization and punctuation.

This bridge was built on _______ .

E8 ● March 6, 1897

Ⓖ march 6, 1897

Ⓗ March 6 1897

Ⓙ march, 6, 1897

This one has been done for you.
Do numbers 19-21 the same way.

17 Ⓐ Jasper helped his mother do the grocery shopping.

Ⓑ The store was very crowded because of the holiday

Ⓒ Mrs. tolliver goes shopping once a week.

Ⓓ they quickly filled a cart.

18 Ⓕ This homework is'nt due until next week.

Ⓖ Lonni wont' be able to study with us tonight.

Ⓗ This answer cant be right.

Ⓙ Marcellus didn't finish his homework yet.

(19) _______

(20) _______

The skates you sent me are wonderful. Thank you for remembering my birthday.

(21) _______

Annie

Directions: Look at the letter. Choose the phrase that fits in the blank and is capitalized and punctuated correctly.

19 Ⓐ august 10, 1996

Ⓑ August 10, 1996

Ⓒ August 10 1996

Ⓓ August 10 1996,

20 Ⓕ Dear Grandfather,

Ⓖ Dear Grandfather.

Ⓗ Dear grandfather,

Ⓙ Dear Grandfather

21 Ⓐ love

Ⓑ Love.

Ⓒ Love,

Ⓓ Love

GO

22

Alice Walters
19 Redbud Street
____

Ⓕ atlanta, Georgia 30314
Ⓖ Atlanta Georgia 30314
Ⓗ atlanta, georgia 30314
Ⓙ Atlanta, Georgia 30314

Directions: Look at the underlined part of the sentence. Fill in the circle for the answer choice that shows the correct capitalization and punctuation for the underlined part.

Did anyone find my hat i lost it yesterday

E9 Ⓐ hat. i
Ⓑ hat. I
Ⓒ hat I
Ⓓ Correct

Do numbers 23-25 the same way.

(23) Mindoro was looking forward to her trip she
(24) was going to go from Chicago to Los Angeles by
train. Her mother and her brother Adrian were
going with her. They would leave on June 28 and
(25) return by plane on july 15

23 Ⓐ trip She
Ⓑ trip. she
Ⓒ trip. She
Ⓓ correct

24 Ⓕ from chicago
Ⓖ from chicago.
Ⓗ from Chicago.
Ⓙ correct

25 Ⓐ July 15.
Ⓑ July 15?
Ⓒ july 15.
Ⓓ correct

STOP

E1 Directions: Choose the word that goes in the blank.

Your watch is _______ than mine.

Ⓐ newest

Ⓑ new

Ⓒ more newer

● newer

This one has been done for you. Do numbers 1–3 the same way.

E2 Directions: Which sentence is written correctly and is a complete sentence?

Ⓕ The phone in the kitchen.

● Arnie called his friends.

Ⓗ Inviting friends to his house for dinner.

Ⓙ Board games after dinner.

This one has been done for you. Do numbers 4–6 the same way.

1 My friend's toy _______ looks almost real.

Ⓐ truck

Ⓑ trucks

2 The wind _______ .

Ⓕ and kites in the sky

Ⓖ stronger than yesterday

Ⓗ blew the door shut

Ⓙ through the trees

3 Lauren and Ralph went to a science fair on Saturday.

Ⓐ He

Ⓑ They

Ⓒ She

4 Ⓕ Claire is oldest than Dan.

Ⓖ Ann has lived next to Kathy for a longest time.

Ⓗ We go for a walk earliest on Sunday.

Ⓙ The joke she told was funny.

5 Ⓐ Many people like to swim.

Ⓑ Fred enjoy drawing and painting.

Ⓒ My sister have a coin collection.

Ⓓ Dylan look for unusual rocks.

6 Ⓕ A porch beside the kitchen.

Ⓖ My bedroom with a window over the park.

Ⓗ The television is in the family room.

STOP

Directions: Look at these sentences.

E3 Which choice is not written correctly?

Ⓐ Where is the can opener?

● It isn't nowhere in this

Ⓒ drawer, and I need it.

This one has been done for you.
Do numbers 7 and 8 the same way.

E4 Find the answer choice that is a complete sentence.

Ⓕ Was in the library.

Ⓖ Two new shirts.

Ⓗ I can't hear you.

Practice on this one.
Do numbers 9 and 10 the same way.

7 Ⓐ The children waited

Ⓑ for the bread to bake.

Ⓒ They knowed it would be good.

8 Ⓕ The mother cat she

Ⓖ wouldn't let any of us

Ⓗ pick up her kittens.

9 Ⓐ Lola walked down the street.

Ⓑ Under the dining room table.

Ⓒ Climbed the ladder to the roof.

10 Ⓕ A loud sound.

Ⓖ He ran quickly.

Ⓗ Waiting in line.

Look at this paragraph.

My sister's name is Karen.
She is three years old than I am.
(1)
We do many things together.
She taught me how to jump rope.
We jump rope with our friends every day.
Karen is teaching me to play basketball.
Our house is in the city.

Look at the underlined word. How should it be written? If you think it is correct, choose correct.

11 Ⓐ oldest

Ⓑ older

Ⓒ correct

Which sentence does not belong in this paragraph?

12 Ⓕ We do many things together.

Ⓖ Karen is teaching me to play basketball.

Ⓗ Our house is in the city.

Directions: Choose the sentence that best fits in this paragraph.

E5 The store clerk helped us. ____________________ . My mother bought new shoes for work.

Ⓐ It is a big store.

Ⓑ My mother works in a bank.

Ⓒ I like shopping with my mother.

● He showed us different shoes.

This one has been done for you.

Do numbers 13–15 the same way.

13 Diana was walking down the street. She saw a can on the ground. ____________________ .

Ⓐ Cars were in the street.

Ⓑ She picked it up and threw it in the trash.

Ⓒ It was Bridge Street.

Ⓓ Diana goes to school with me.

14 ____________________ . We decided to have a snack. My father gave us apples and bananas.

Ⓕ After school my brother and I were hungry.

Ⓖ School was fun today.

Ⓗ My father works at home.

Ⓙ I get home from school about three o'clock.

15 A bird landed in the tree. ____________________ . Then it flew away to another tree.

Ⓐ There are many trees in the park.

Ⓑ Birds have feathers.

Ⓒ It sang a pretty song for a few minutes.

Ⓓ Birds build nests and lay eggs.

STOP

Cecil is writing a story about a trip his family took. He made this chart to plan his story. Which idea does not belong in the story?

16

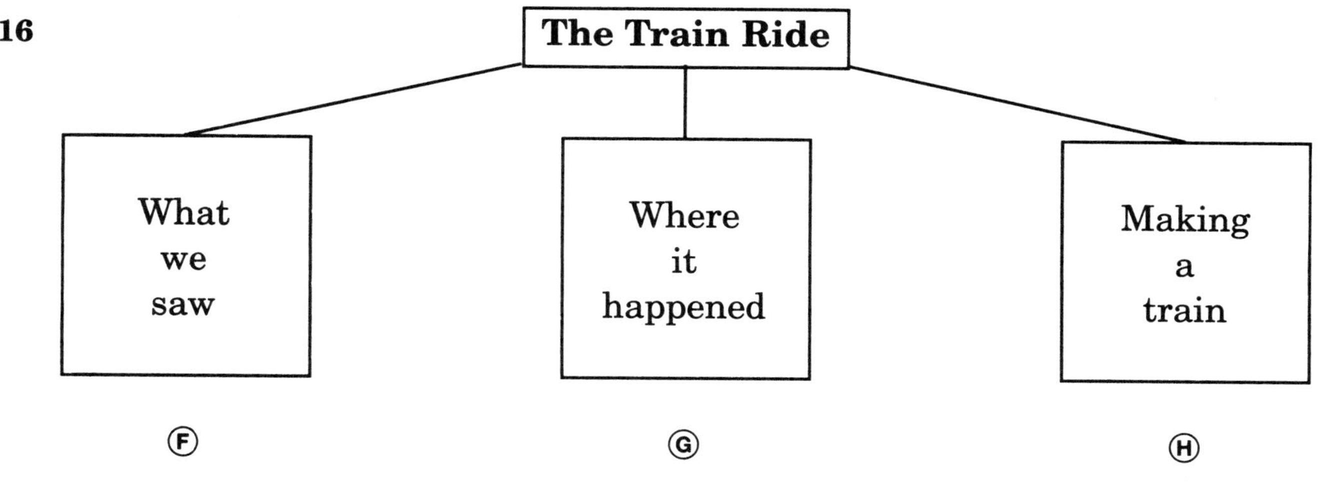

The Train Ride

Last summer my family went to Colorado.
We took a ride on an old train.
It went from Durango to Silverton.
Our trip lasted three weeks.
The tracks went right through the mountains.
The mountains were still covered with snow.

Which sentence should Cecil use to end his story?

17 Ⓐ We saw many birds and animals.

Ⓑ My mother liked it.

Ⓒ It usually snows in winter.

Which sentence should Cecil leave out of his story?

18 Ⓕ We took a ride on an old train.

Ⓖ Our trip lasted three weeks.

Ⓗ The tracks went right through the mountains.

STOP

Part 4 Spelling

Directions: Which word fits in the blank and is spelled correctly?

E1 My mother will _______ to Rome. Ⓐ flie ● fly Ⓑ fley Ⓓ fliy This one has been done for you.	**E2** Will you meet us _______ ? Ⓕ latir Ⓗ layter Ⓖ laitir Ⓙ later Practice on this one.

Do numbers 1–10 the same way.

1 My apartment is _______ hers.

Ⓐ bilow Ⓒ belo
Ⓑ below Ⓓ balow

2 The car cost too _______ .

Ⓕ much Ⓗ muche
Ⓖ mutch Ⓙ moch

3 The _______ on the beach was very hot.

Ⓐ cand Ⓒ sand
Ⓑ sant Ⓓ scand

4 Can you _______ these shoes?

Ⓕ repare Ⓗ repair
Ⓖ ripair Ⓙ repar

5 Don't _______ without me.

Ⓐ start Ⓒ sdart
Ⓑ stard Ⓓ stert

6 Nadia heard a _______ sound.

Ⓕ strainge Ⓗ strang
Ⓖ strange Ⓙ straing

7 Juan, your sister is _______ .

Ⓐ here Ⓒ hier
Ⓑ heer Ⓓ heere

8 Does she _______ to the club?

Ⓕ belong Ⓗ belawng
Ⓖ bilong Ⓙ bellong

9 I'm sure we will _______ it.

Ⓐ fynd Ⓒ feind
Ⓑ finde Ⓓ find

10 The _______ will close at nine.

Ⓕ markit Ⓗ market
Ⓖ merkit Ⓙ marcket

STOP

Directions: Which word in each group is not spelled correctly?

E3	E4
like Ⓐ roll Ⓑ soop ● (C) This one has been done for you.	Ⓕ quick Ⓖ lend Ⓗ ask Ⓙ sweap Practice on this one.

Do numbers 11–18 the same way.

11

return Ⓐ   camra Ⓑ   friend Ⓒ

12

hope Ⓕ   shoe Ⓖ   stoor Ⓗ

13

pik Ⓐ   end Ⓑ   rope Ⓒ

14

think Ⓕ   hors Ⓖ   wild Ⓗ

15
- Ⓐ poal
- Ⓑ breeze
- Ⓒ making
- Ⓓ clear

16
- Ⓕ shout
- Ⓖ line
- Ⓗ poynt
- Ⓙ foot

17
- Ⓐ tell
- Ⓑ clowd
- Ⓒ sky
- Ⓓ rest

18
- Ⓕ bike
- Ⓖ print
- Ⓗ sheep
- Ⓙ nise

STOP

Directions: Look at the underlined words in each sentence. Which one is spelled incorrectly?

E5 Wich of these brushes is yours?

Ⓐ Ⓑ Ⓒ

Practice on this one.
Do numbers 19–25 the same way.

19 Nancy had a grait idea about how to fix the broken toy.

Ⓐ Ⓑ Ⓒ

20 What does this word mene?

Ⓕ Ⓖ Ⓗ

21 At the party Reggie will sirve fresh fruit.

Ⓐ Ⓑ Ⓒ

22 Using a spune is the best way to eat soup.

Ⓕ Ⓖ Ⓗ

23 Be careful not to spill anythin on your coat.

Ⓐ Ⓑ Ⓒ

24 A blak dog picked up the ball in his mouth.

Ⓕ Ⓖ Ⓗ

25 Many people fly kites on a wendy day.

Ⓐ Ⓑ Ⓒ

STOP

Part 5 Study Skills

Directions: Look at these definitions. Then answer the questions. The first one has been done for you.

recover
To get better after being sick or injured

E1 How do you spell a word that means "to get better"?

Ⓐ ricover

Ⓑ recovir

● recover

gaze
To look at for a long time

snorkel
A device that allows you to breathe under water

trunk
A large chest for storing things

wrench
A tool used for gripping and turning

Do numbers 1 and 2 the same way.

1 Who is most likely to use a wrench?

Ⓐ a plumber

Ⓑ a skin diver

Ⓒ a doctor

2 Where would you use a snorkel?

Ⓕ on a mountain

Ⓖ in a desert

Ⓗ in a lake

This table of contents is from a book about dogs.

Table of Contents

1. The First Dogs 1
2. Kinds of Dogs 8
3. Dogs That Work 19
4. Training Dogs 27
5. Taking Care of Dogs 40

If you wanted to learn to train a dog, which page should you turn to?

3 Ⓐ 19

Ⓑ 27

Ⓒ 40

If you start reading on page 40, what will you read about?

4 Ⓕ brushing dogs

Ⓖ teaching dogs to sit

Ⓗ hunting dogs

ALDAN SCHOOL

NORTH

Playground

Room 104

Room 103

Room 102

Room 101

Cafeteria

Gym

Computer Center

Library

Office

Nurse

Storage

WEST

Ninth Street

Tenth Street

EAST

Aldan Street

SOUTH

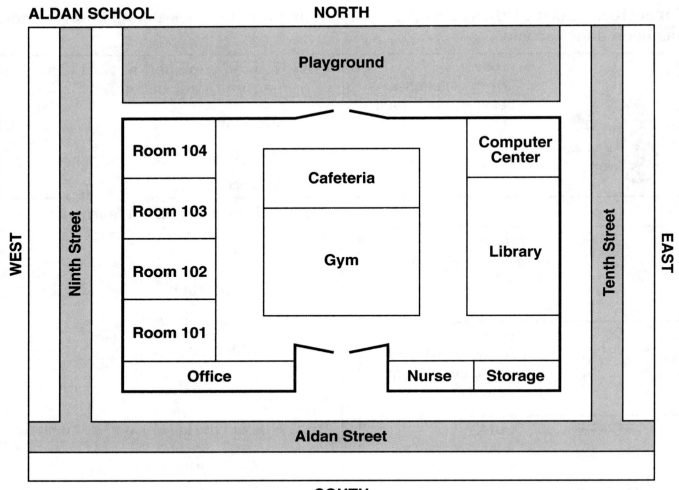

Directions: Answer the questions about this map.

5 What street is west of the school?

Ⓐ Aldan Street

Ⓑ Ninth Street

Ⓒ Tenth Street

6 Which is beside the library?

Ⓕ the Computer Center

Ⓖ the Office

Ⓗ Room 104

7 If you walked north from the cafeteria, where would you be?

Ⓐ in the Gym

Ⓑ in the Library

Ⓒ in the Playground

8 Which is closest to the office?

Ⓕ Room 104

Ⓖ Room 101

Ⓗ the Computer Center

Table of Contents

Math

Lesson 1 Numeration

Example **Directions:** Read or listen to the question. Then choose the best answer. This one has been done for you.

A How many dots are there?

10 Ⓐ   64 Ⓑ   46 ●

Read or listen carefully to the problem and think about what to do before you choose an answer.

Practice

1 Which number is between 50 and 57?

56 Ⓐ   58 Ⓑ   49 Ⓒ   59 Ⓓ

2 Which number is the expanded numeral for nine hundred thirty-four?

9 + 100 + 34 Ⓕ   9 + 100 + 34 Ⓖ   900 + 30 + 4 Ⓗ   93 + 4 Ⓙ

3 Which record is fourth from the guitar?

Ⓐ Ⓑ Ⓒ Ⓓ

4 What numbers should go in the blank spaces when you count by ones?

42, 43, ___ , 45, 46, ___

44 and 48 Ⓕ   41 and 47 Ⓖ   44 and 47 Ⓗ   41 and 48 Ⓙ

GO

5 There are 45 books in the box. Each shelf holds ten books. How many shelves can be filled completely with books?

10	9	4	5
Ⓐ	Ⓑ	Ⓒ	Ⓓ

6 Look at the group of matches. Which group of needles has the same number as there are matches?

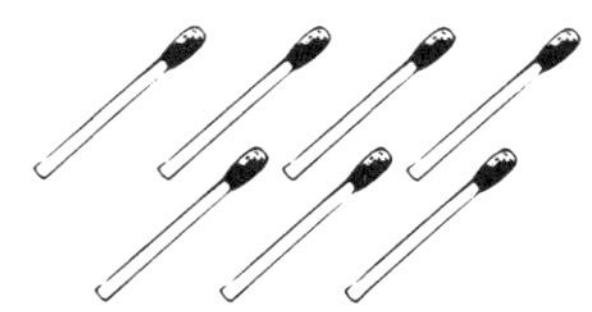

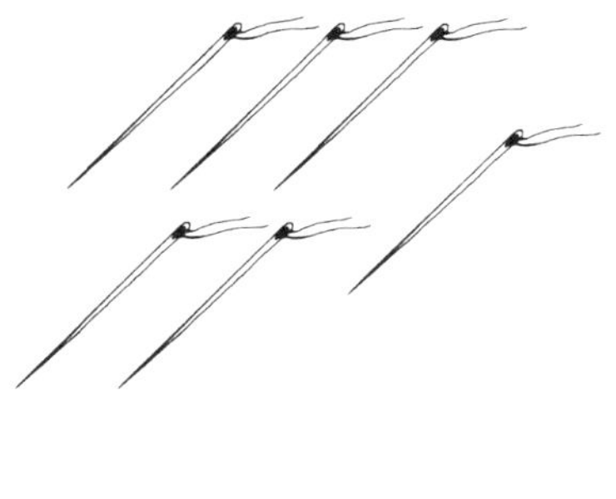
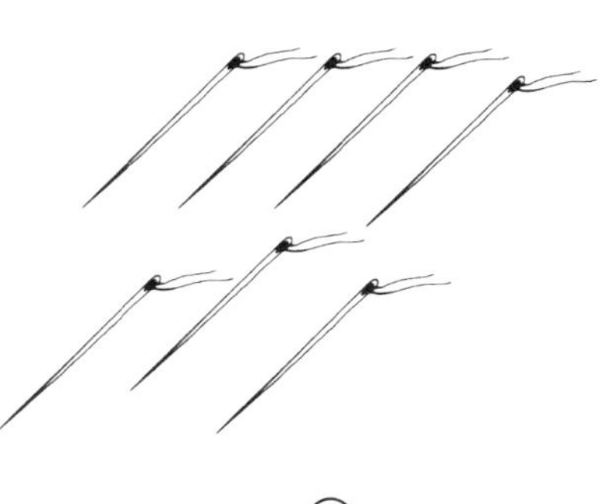
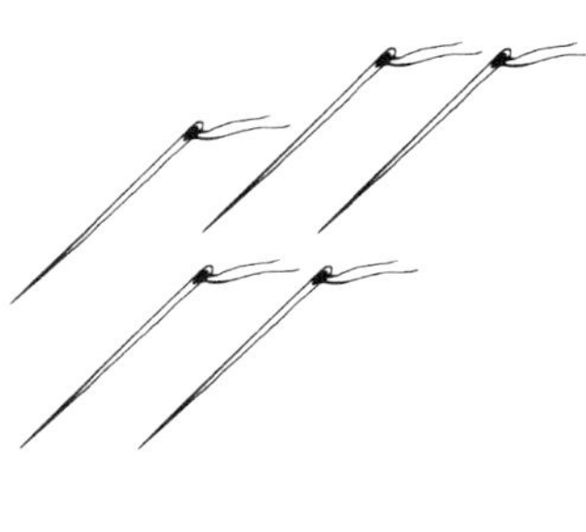

Ⓕ Ⓖ Ⓗ

7 What numeral should replace the circle on the number line?

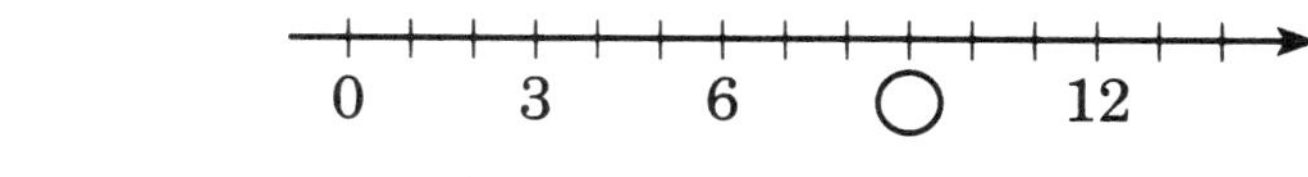

9	8	11	10
Ⓐ	Ⓑ	Ⓒ	Ⓓ

8 Which numeral shows the difference between 3 and 10?

6	13	5	7
Ⓕ	Ⓖ	Ⓗ	Ⓙ

9 Mark the group that shows numbers in correct counting order.

59, 58, 60, 61	58, 59, 60, 61	58, 59, 61, 60	58, 59, 63, 61
Ⓐ	Ⓑ	Ⓒ	Ⓓ

STOP

Example **Directions:** Read or listen to the question. Then choose the correct answer.

A This one has been done for you. Which numeral matches the word?

sixty

16	60	6	66
Ⓐ	●	Ⓒ	Ⓓ

Look at all the answer choices before you mark the one you think is correct.

Practice

1 What number word goes in the blank in the box?

fifteen, sixteen, ____________, eighteen

seventeen	nineteen	fourteen	twenty
Ⓐ	Ⓑ	Ⓒ	Ⓓ

2 What number is eight hundred ninety-two?

8092	928	892	829
Ⓕ	Ⓖ	Ⓗ	Ⓙ

3 What number matches the word in the box?

six thousand, one hundred

1006	610	60,100	6100
Ⓐ	Ⓑ	Ⓒ	Ⓓ

4 What word matches the number in the middle of the box?

9, 10, 11, 12, 13

twelve	eleven	ten	nine
Ⓕ	Ⓖ	Ⓗ	Ⓙ

GO

5 What number is three hundred seventy-one?

371	317	3071	3701
Ⓐ	Ⓑ	Ⓒ	Ⓓ

6 Which number matches the word in the box?

seven hundred fourteen

741	7014	714	700,014
Ⓕ	Ⓖ	Ⓗ	Ⓙ

7 Which number is two-thousand three-hundred seventy?

2730	2370	2307	200,370
Ⓐ	Ⓑ	Ⓒ	Ⓓ

8 Which number matches the word in the box?

eighty-six

860	806	68	86
Ⓕ	Ⓖ	Ⓗ	Ⓙ

9 If you are counting by ones, what number word should go in the box?

nineteen, ____________, twenty-one, twenty-two

twenty-three	eighteen	twenty	seventeen
Ⓐ	Ⓑ	Ⓒ	Ⓓ

10 What word stands for the number in the box?

52

twenty-five	fifty-two	fifty	fifty-three
Ⓕ	Ⓖ	Ⓗ	Ⓙ

STOP

Example **Directions:** Read or listen to the question. Then choose the best answer. This one has been done for you.

A Which pattern shows counting by twos?

2, 5, 8	3, 6, 9	20, 21, 22	8, 10, 12
Ⓐ	Ⓑ	Ⓒ	●

If you are not sure which answer choice is correct, take your best guess.

Practice

1 Look at the hundreds, tens, and ones chart. Which number is represented by the dots on the chart?

100s	10s	1
● ● ● ● ● ●	● ●	● ● ●

6023	623	6003	632
Ⓐ	Ⓑ	Ⓒ	Ⓓ

2 Which digit is in the hundreds place?

5019

1	5	9	0
Ⓕ	Ⓖ	Ⓗ	Ⓙ

3 Which figure is one-third shaded?

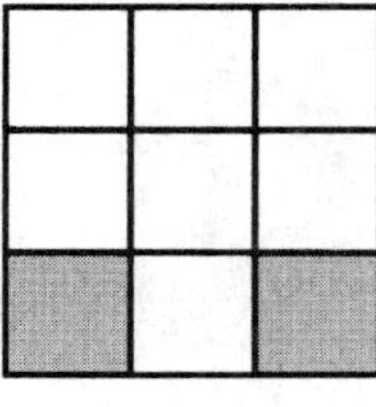
Ⓐ

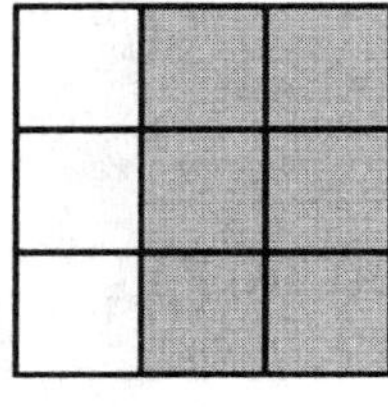
Ⓑ

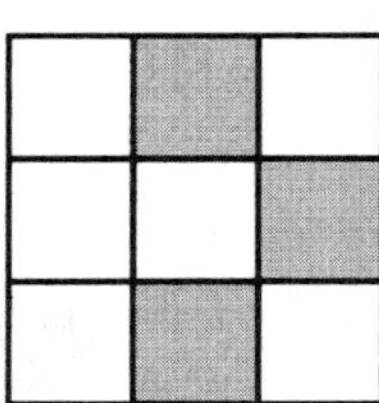
Ⓒ

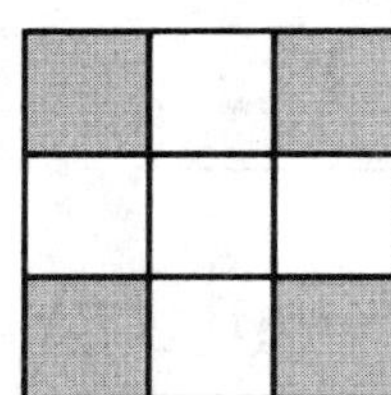
Ⓓ

GO

4 What number should go in the empty circle?

48	45	49	47
Ⓕ	Ⓖ	Ⓗ	Ⓙ

5 Look at the pattern. Choose the picture below that should come next in the pattern.

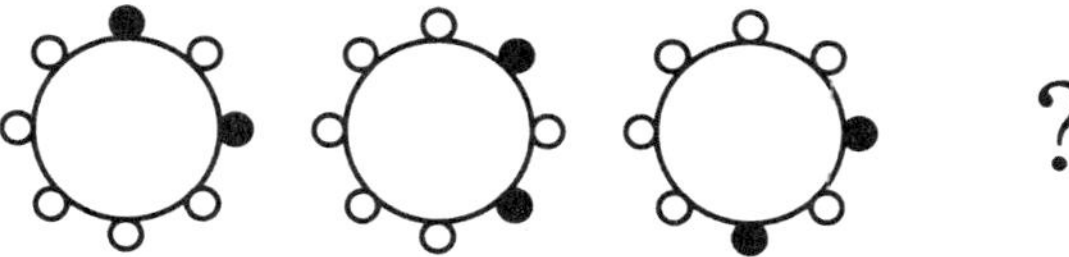

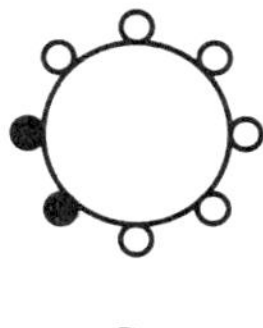

Ⓐ

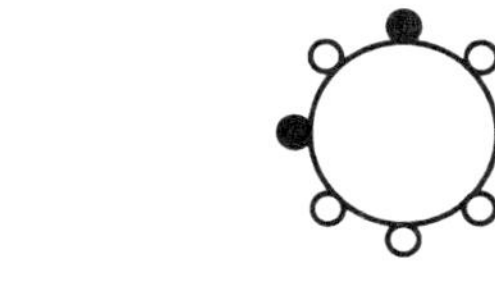

Ⓑ Ⓒ

Ⓓ

6 Look at the numbers in the box. Which one below does *not* belong in the box?

24, 28, 30, 32, 36, 38

30	28	36	32
Ⓕ	Ⓖ	Ⓗ	Ⓙ

7 Look at the number in the box. What is the place value of seven?

275

ones	hundreds	tens
Ⓐ	Ⓑ	Ⓒ

8 Which number has 8 ones and 5 hundreds?

58	518	580	805
Ⓕ	Ⓖ	Ⓗ	Ⓙ

9 Look at the pattern. Which numbers are missing from the pattern?

58, 61, 64, ___ , ___

67, 70	66, 68	65, 68
Ⓐ	Ⓑ	Ⓒ

Example **Directions:** Read or listen to the question. Then choose the best answer. This one has been done for you.

A Look at the number sentence in the box. Which sign will make the sentence true?

10 ○ 5 = 5

÷	×	+	−
Ⓐ	Ⓑ	Ⓒ	●

Look carefully at the answer choices. Be sure you fill in the space under the one you think is correct.

Practice

1 How many problems have an answer equal to five?

$$\begin{array}{r}8\\+\ 4\\\hline\end{array}\quad\begin{array}{r}8\\-\ 3\\\hline\end{array}\quad\begin{array}{r}2\\+\ 3\\\hline\end{array}\quad\begin{array}{r}9\\-\ 4\\\hline\end{array}\quad\begin{array}{r}1\\+\ 4\\\hline\end{array}$$

1	4	2	3
Ⓐ	Ⓑ	Ⓒ	Ⓓ

2 Which multiplication fact is shown by the dots?

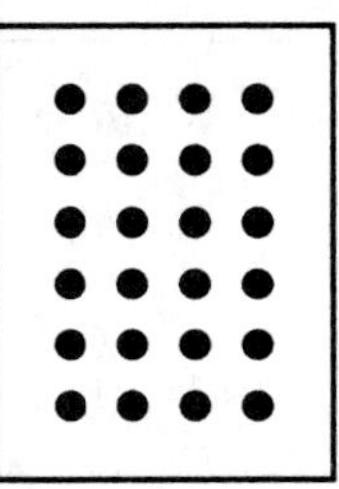

6 × 4 = 24	6 × 5 = 30	5 × 5 = 25	2 × 12 = 24
Ⓕ	Ⓖ	Ⓗ	Ⓙ

3 Which group of number statements means the same as the one in the box?

nine

4 + 4	10 − 2	2 + 7	13 − 8
12 − 4	6 + 4	14 − 5	2 + 8
Ⓐ	Ⓑ	Ⓒ	Ⓓ

GO

4 What is another way to write eight is less than twelve?

$8 = 12$ Ⓕ

$12 > 8$ Ⓖ

$8 > 12$ Ⓗ

$8 \div 12$ Ⓙ

---

5 Six bees leave the hive. Then five more bees leave the hive. Find the number sentence that shows how many bees in all left the hive.

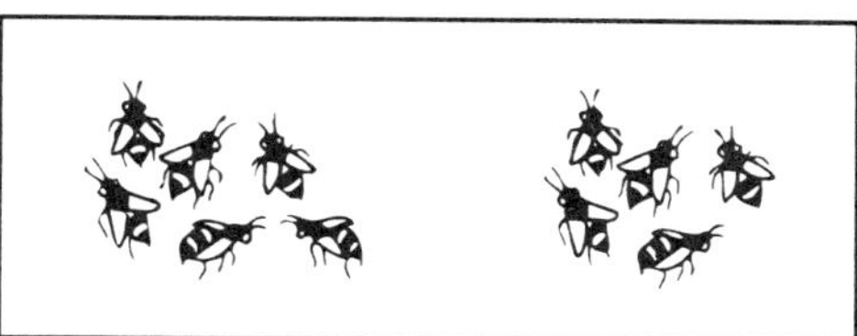

$6 + 5 = 11$ Ⓐ

$6 - 5 = 1$ Ⓑ

$11 - 6 = 5$ Ⓒ

$11 - 5 = 6$ Ⓓ

---

6 Look at the numbers in the table. The "in" numbers have been changed in some way to "out" numbers that are different. How are the "in" numbers changed?

IN	OUT
4	11
6	13
12	19

add 13 Ⓕ

add 9 Ⓖ

add 6 Ⓗ

add 7 Ⓙ

---

7 What is forty-two rounded to the nearest ten?

10 Ⓐ

50 Ⓑ

40 Ⓒ

45 Ⓓ

---

8 Look at the number sentence in the box. What is the best estimate of your answer?

$185 + 97 = \square$

200 Ⓕ

300 Ⓖ

150 Ⓗ

250 Ⓙ

STOP

Directions: Read or listen to the question. Then choose the best answer. This one has been done for you.

E1 Twenty people are in line for the bus. Joan is twelfth in line. How many people are behind Joan?

12	20	9	8
Ⓐ	Ⓑ	Ⓒ	●

1 Look at the shapes. Find the fraction that tells what part of the shapes are squares.

 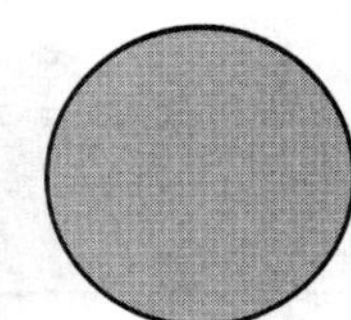  

$\frac{1}{2}$	$\frac{1}{4}$	$\frac{3}{4}$	$\frac{2}{3}$
Ⓐ	Ⓑ	Ⓒ	Ⓓ

2 Which answer shows how many tens and ones are in thirty-five?

3 tens 5 ones	5 tens 3 ones	3 tens 4 ones	5 tens 6 ones
Ⓕ	Ⓖ	Ⓗ	Ⓙ

3 Which number is the same as the squares in the box?

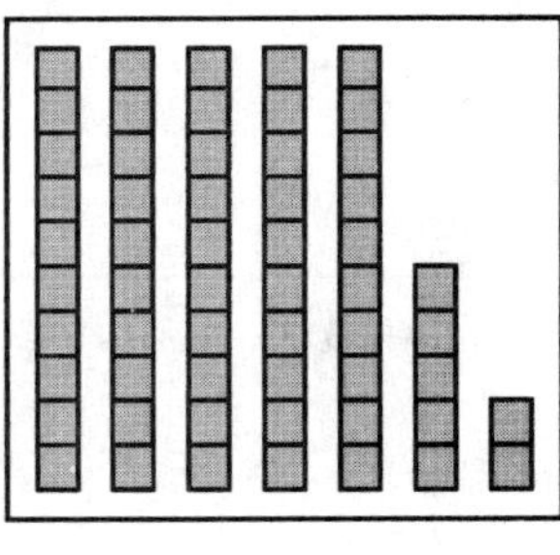

552	62	57	75
Ⓐ	Ⓑ	Ⓒ	Ⓓ

4 Which number has an eight in the hundreds place?

873	738	783	788
Ⓕ	Ⓖ	Ⓗ	Ⓙ

GO

5 What number is shown in the hundreds, tens, and ones chart?

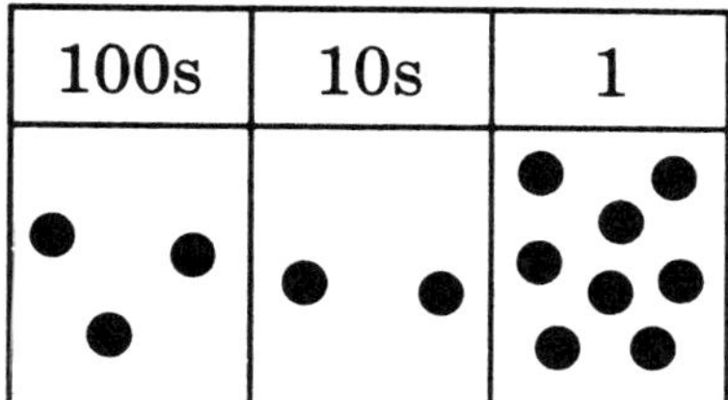

823	328	238	382
Ⓐ	Ⓑ	Ⓒ	Ⓓ

6 What numeral should replace the square?

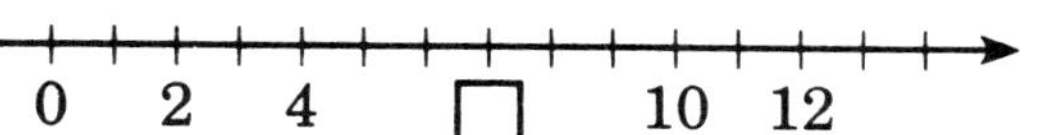

5	8	7	9
Ⓕ	Ⓖ	Ⓗ	Ⓙ

7 Which number is two-hundred and twenty-nine?

292	299	992	229
Ⓐ	Ⓑ	Ⓒ	Ⓓ

8 What numeral is between 67 and 98?

80	50	99	63
Ⓕ	Ⓖ	Ⓗ	Ⓙ

9 What number means five hundreds, one ten, four ones?

541	514	510	544
Ⓐ	Ⓑ	Ⓒ	Ⓓ

10 In which group are both numbers in the circles larger than both numbers in the squares?

Squares: 12, 9	Squares: 12, 10	Squares: 9, 6	Squares: 12, 6
Circles: 10, 6	Circles: 9, 6	Circles: 10, 12	Circles: 9, 10
Ⓕ	Ⓖ	Ⓗ	Ⓙ

GO

11 What number should go in the box to make both sentences true?

$$8 + \square = 11$$

$$11 - \square = 8$$

18 Ⓐ 19 Ⓑ 2 Ⓒ 3 Ⓓ

---

12 Which shape is missing from the pattern in the box?

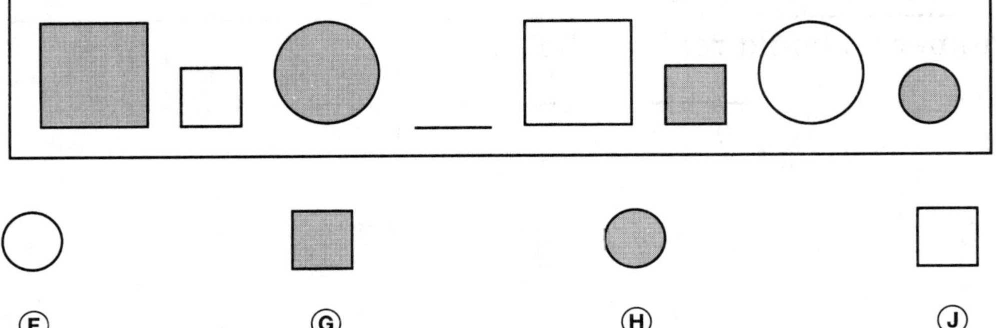

Ⓕ Ⓖ Ⓗ Ⓙ

---

13 Look at the numbers in the chart. The "in" numbers are changed in some way to different numbers when they come out. How are the "in" numbers changed?

IN	OUT
9	5
14	10
20	16

subtract 6 Ⓐ add 6 Ⓑ subtract 4 Ⓒ add 4 Ⓓ

---

14 Look at the shapes. Mark the circle under the shape that is one-half shaded.

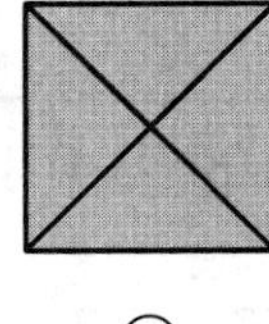 Ⓕ

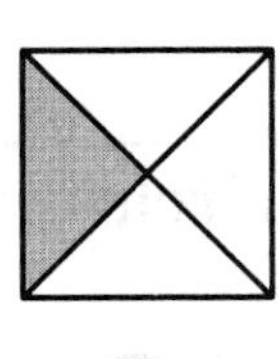 Ⓖ

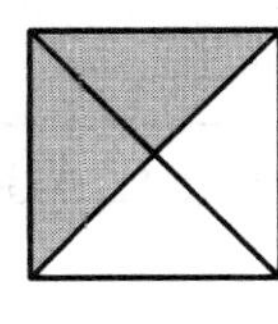 Ⓗ

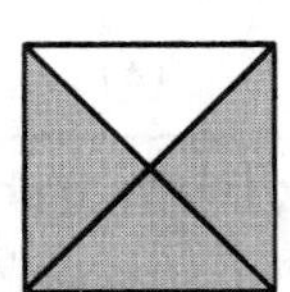 Ⓙ

---

15 What is another way to write 12 is less than 20?

$20 + 12$ Ⓐ $20 > 12$ Ⓑ $12 > 20$ Ⓒ $20 < 12$ Ⓓ

GO

16 This boat holds 95 passengers. At dinner, ten passengers sit at each table. If all the passengers come to dinner, how many tables will they fill completely?

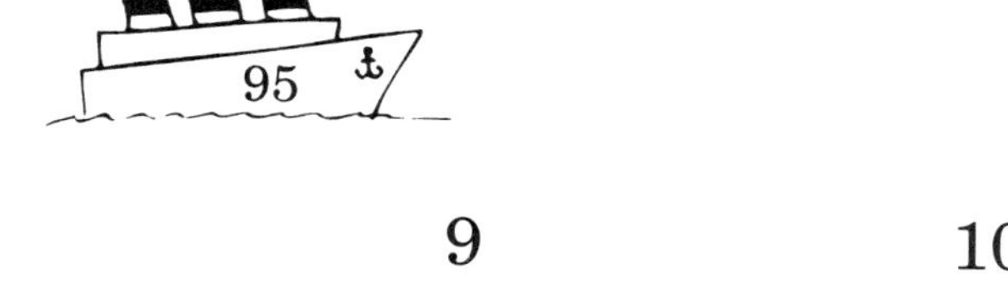

8	5	9	10
Ⓕ	Ⓖ	Ⓗ	Ⓙ

17 How many problems below have the answer ten?

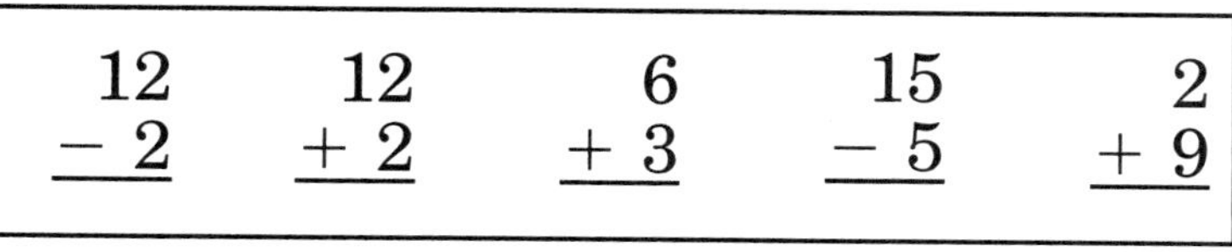

$12 - 2$ $12 + 2$ $6 + 3$ $15 - 5$ $2 + 9$

1	2	3	4
Ⓐ	Ⓑ	Ⓒ	Ⓓ

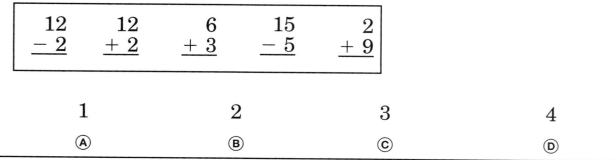

18 Which symbol is needed to make the number sentence true?

$4 + 7 = 15 \square 4$

$-$	$+$	$\div$	$\times$
Ⓕ	Ⓖ	Ⓗ	Ⓙ

19 What number is missing?

12, 18, ___ , 30, 36

22	26	20	24
Ⓐ	Ⓑ	Ⓒ	Ⓓ

20 Which number is the best estimate of the correct answer to the number sentence?

$$513 - 189 = \square$$

250	300	700	150
Ⓕ	Ⓖ	Ⓗ	Ⓙ

STOP

NUMBER RIGHT ______

Lesson 6 Addition

Example **Directions:** Solve each addition problem. Choose the best answer.

A This one has been done for you.		**B** Practice on this one.	
	6 Ⓐ		28 Ⓕ
9	12 ●		16 Ⓖ
+ 3	13 Ⓒ	22 + 6 = □	82 Ⓗ
	39 Ⓓ		38 Ⓙ

If a problem is too difficult, skip it and come back to it later if you have time.

Do numbers 1-14 the same way.

Practice

1

33¢
+ 31¢

66¢ Ⓐ
44¢ Ⓑ
74¢ Ⓒ
64¢ Ⓓ

2

15 + 32 = □

47 Ⓕ
37 Ⓖ
17 Ⓗ
83 Ⓙ

3

318 + 61 = □

369 Ⓐ
342 Ⓑ
257 Ⓒ
379 Ⓓ

4

49 + 25 = □

76 Ⓕ
74 Ⓖ
24 Ⓗ
64 Ⓙ

5

12
7
+ 4

29 Ⓐ
13 Ⓑ
19 Ⓒ
23 Ⓓ

6

4
4
+ 4

44 Ⓕ
14 Ⓖ
12 Ⓗ
8 Ⓙ

GO

7

$$\begin{array}{r} 362 \\ +571 \\ \hline \end{array}$$

897 Ⓐ
879 Ⓑ
833 Ⓒ
933 Ⓓ

8

$34 + 23 = \square$

57 Ⓕ
66 Ⓖ
47 Ⓗ
56 Ⓙ

9

$40 + 80 =$

122 Ⓐ
120 Ⓑ
130 Ⓒ
148 Ⓓ

10

$7 + 9 + 6 =$

22 Ⓕ
16 Ⓖ
15 Ⓗ
25 Ⓙ

11

$$\begin{array}{r} 9 \\ +5 \\ \hline \end{array}$$

14 Ⓐ
59 Ⓑ
4 Ⓒ
13 Ⓓ

12

$$\begin{array}{r} 8 \\ +35 \\ \hline \end{array}$$

23 Ⓕ
27 Ⓖ
43 Ⓗ
115 Ⓙ

13

$$\begin{array}{r} 10 \\ 75 \\ +18 \\ \hline \end{array}$$

115 Ⓐ
93 Ⓑ
85 Ⓒ
103 Ⓓ

14

$\square + 8 = 16$

7 Ⓕ
6 Ⓖ
8 Ⓗ
24 Ⓙ

STOP

Example **Directions:** Solve each subtraction problem. Choose the right answer.

This one has been done for you.		Practice on this one.	
	8 ●		11 Ⓕ
10	12 Ⓑ	$19 - 6 = \square$	25 Ⓖ
− 2	7 Ⓒ		59 Ⓗ
	10 Ⓓ		13 Ⓙ

Do numbers 1-14 the same way.

If you cannot find the answer to a problem, take your best guess and move on to the next problem.

Practice

1

$94 - 34 = \square$

64 Ⓐ
128 Ⓑ
60 Ⓒ
40 Ⓓ

2

$$\begin{array}{r} 44 \\ -\ 3 \\ \hline \end{array}$$

14 Ⓕ
47 Ⓖ
31 Ⓗ
41 Ⓙ

3

$$\begin{array}{r} 90 \\ -\ 55 \\ \hline \end{array}$$

45 Ⓐ
35 Ⓑ
40 Ⓒ
54 Ⓓ

4

$477 - 83 = \square$

560 Ⓕ
394 Ⓖ
294 Ⓗ
414 Ⓙ

5

$31 - 14 = \square$

17 Ⓐ
7 Ⓑ
27 Ⓒ
21 Ⓓ

6

$563 - 7 = \square$

513 Ⓕ
570 Ⓖ
546 Ⓗ
556 Ⓙ

GO

7

$$\begin{array}{r} 402 \\ -\ 58 \\ \hline \end{array}$$

90 Ⓐ
456 Ⓑ
344 Ⓒ
11 Ⓓ

8

$$\begin{array}{r} 52¢ \\ -\ 19¢ \\ \hline \end{array}$$

71¢ Ⓕ
33¢ Ⓖ
43¢ Ⓗ
14¢ Ⓙ

9

$8 - 3 = \square$

11 Ⓐ
4 Ⓑ
12 Ⓒ
5 Ⓓ

10

$$\begin{array}{r} 50 \\ -\ 10 \\ \hline \end{array}$$

30 Ⓕ
40 Ⓖ
15 Ⓗ
10 Ⓙ

11

$267 - 81 = \square$

348 Ⓐ
186 Ⓑ
286 Ⓒ
226 Ⓓ

12

$$\begin{array}{r} 644 \\ -\ 77 \\ \hline \end{array}$$

567 Ⓕ
633 Ⓖ
577 Ⓗ
721 Ⓙ

13

$$\begin{array}{r} 856 \\ -411 \\ \hline \end{array}$$

345 Ⓐ
434 Ⓑ
454 Ⓒ
445 Ⓓ

14

$$\begin{array}{r} 328 \\ -319 \\ \hline \end{array}$$

309 Ⓕ
9 Ⓖ
647 Ⓗ
11 Ⓙ

STOP

Example **Directions:** Choose the right answer to these multiplication and division problems.

This one has been done for you.		Practice on this one.	
	7 Ⓐ		12 Ⓕ
3×4	12 ●	$4 \div 2 = \square$	0 Ⓖ
	1 Ⓒ		2 Ⓗ
	34 Ⓓ		3 Ⓙ

Look carefully at the problem to be sure you are performing the correct operation.

Do numbers 1-6 the same way.

Practice

1

6×4

2 Ⓐ
12 Ⓑ
46 Ⓒ
24 Ⓓ

2

$3 \times 7 = \square$

10 Ⓕ
21 Ⓖ
37 Ⓗ
4 Ⓙ

3

$8 \times 5 = \square$

40 Ⓐ
13 Ⓑ
3 Ⓒ
30 Ⓓ

4

$14 \div 7 = \square$

7 Ⓕ
2 Ⓖ
21 Ⓗ
11 Ⓙ

5

$3\overline{)30}$

13 Ⓐ
1 Ⓑ
20 Ⓒ
10 Ⓓ

6

$15 \div 5 = \square$

20 Ⓕ
4 Ⓖ
3 Ⓗ
10 Ⓙ

STOP

Example **Directions:** Solve each problem. Mark the circle beside the answer you think is correct. If the answer is not shown, choose N for None.

This one has been done for you.	Practice on this one.
1 + 3 = □ 5 Ⓐ 2 Ⓑ 4 ● N Ⓓ	15¢ − 6¢ 9¢ Ⓕ 21¢ Ⓖ 8¢ Ⓗ 22¢ Ⓙ

Do numbers 1-18 the same way.

Practice

1 6 + 6 = □

12 Ⓐ 11 Ⓑ 0 Ⓒ N Ⓓ

2 2 + 5 = □

3 Ⓕ 8 Ⓖ 7 Ⓗ N Ⓙ

3 19 + 4 = □

49 Ⓐ 13 Ⓑ 22 Ⓒ N Ⓓ

4 8 − 7 = □

15 Ⓕ 1 Ⓖ 7 Ⓗ N Ⓙ

5 12 − 2 = □

14 Ⓐ 10 Ⓑ 22 Ⓒ N Ⓓ

6 24 − 6 = □

8 Ⓕ 22 Ⓖ 18 Ⓗ N Ⓙ

7 630 − 80

650 Ⓐ
710 Ⓑ
622 Ⓒ
550 Ⓓ

8 67 + 32 = □

90 Ⓕ
89 Ⓖ
99 Ⓗ
109 Ⓙ

9 8 + 9 + 7

17 Ⓐ
24 Ⓑ
34 Ⓒ
26 Ⓓ

10 273 − 62 = □

211 Ⓕ
201 Ⓖ
111 Ⓗ
235 Ⓙ

GO

11

$3 + 6 + 8 + 5 = \square$

22 Ⓐ
21 Ⓑ
17 Ⓒ
19 Ⓓ

12

$$\begin{array}{r} 93¢ \\ -\ 57¢ \\ \hline \end{array}$$

22¢ Ⓕ
36¢ Ⓖ
46¢ Ⓗ
44¢ Ⓙ

13

$$\begin{array}{r} 699 \\ -\ 447 \\ \hline \end{array}$$

225 Ⓐ
242 Ⓑ
252 Ⓒ
152 Ⓓ

14

$$\begin{array}{r} 40 \\ 16 \\ +\ 62 \\ \hline \end{array}$$

78 Ⓕ
56 Ⓖ
128 Ⓗ
118 Ⓙ

15

$$\begin{array}{r} 7 \\ \times\ 6 \\ \hline \end{array}$$

1 Ⓐ
48 Ⓑ
42 Ⓒ
13 Ⓓ

16

$3 \times 5 = \square$

8 Ⓕ
15 Ⓖ
18 Ⓗ
2 Ⓙ

17

$4\overline{)20}$

5 Ⓐ
80 Ⓑ
16 Ⓒ
6 Ⓓ

18

$18 \div 6 = \square$

24 Ⓕ
4 Ⓖ
3 Ⓗ
12 Ⓙ

STOP

NUMBER RIGHT ______

Lesson 10 Geometry

Example **Directions:** Choose the best answer to each question.

A Which picture looks the most like a cylinder?

Ⓐ

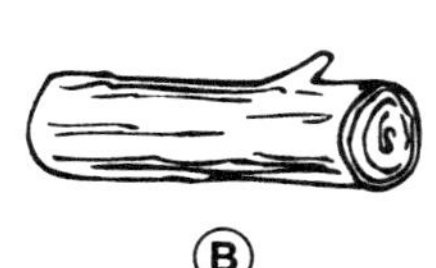
Ⓑ

Ⓒ

Ⓓ

Use key words, pictures, and numbers to help you find the answer.

Practice

1 Which figure has no corners?

rectangle Ⓐ | square Ⓑ | triangle Ⓒ | circle Ⓓ

2 If you folded this figure in half, the two sides will fit together perfectly. Which figure is it?

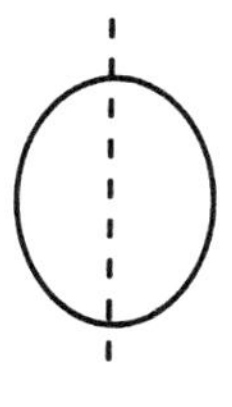
Ⓕ

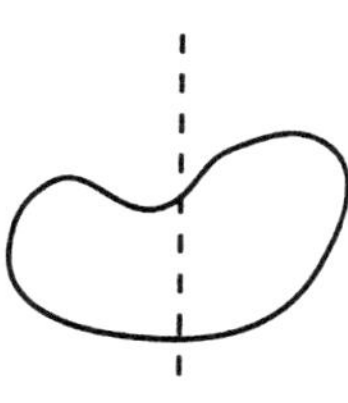
Ⓖ

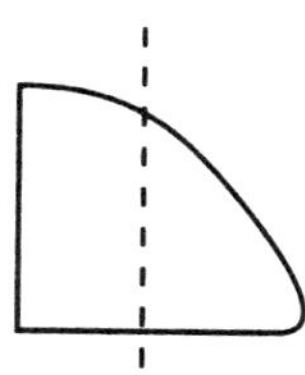
Ⓗ

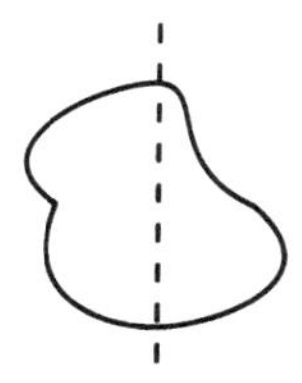
Ⓙ

3 Look at the figure in the box. Which figure has the same size and shape as the one in the box?

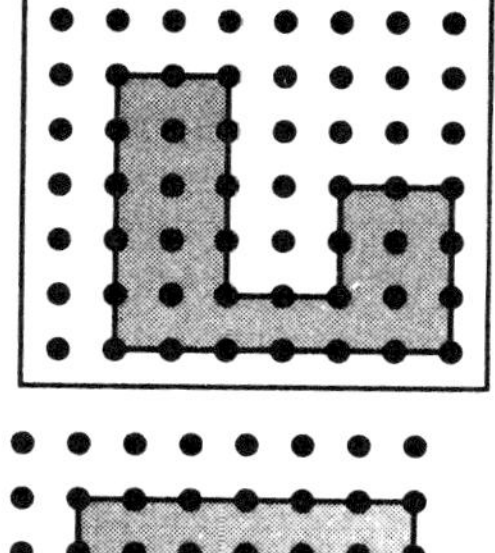

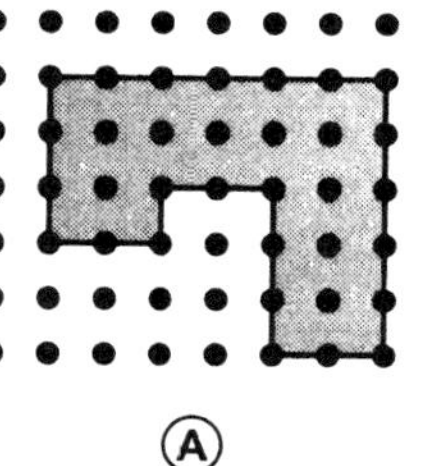
Ⓐ

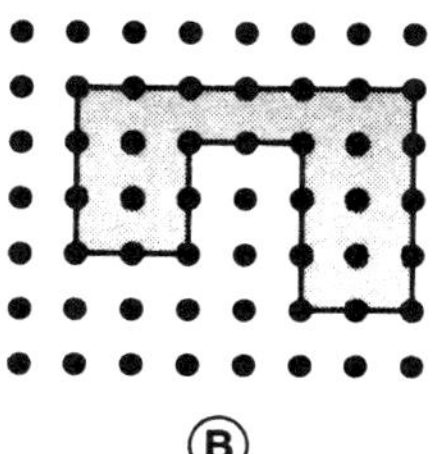
Ⓑ

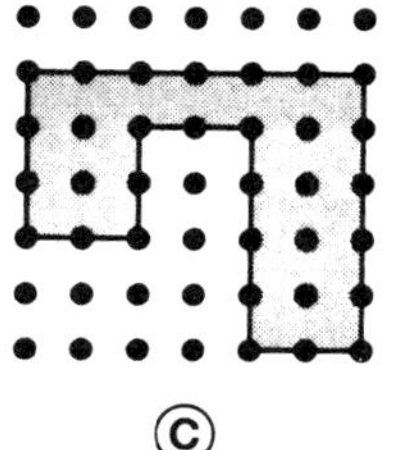
Ⓒ

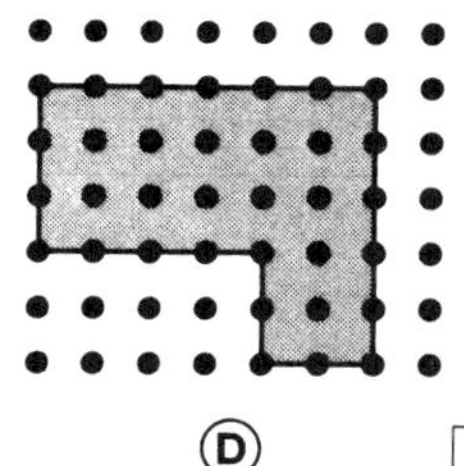
Ⓓ

GO

4 How many of these shapes are spheres?

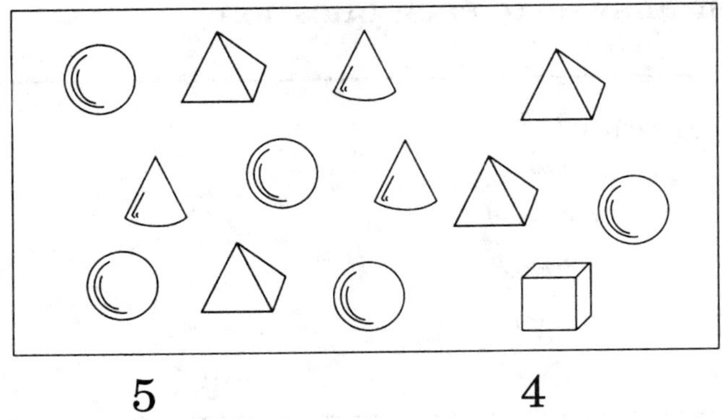

5	4	3	1
Ⓕ	Ⓖ	Ⓗ	Ⓙ

---

5 How many sides does a square have?

3	6	4	8
Ⓐ	Ⓑ	Ⓒ	Ⓓ

---

6 What shape would you have if you cut the ball exactly in half?

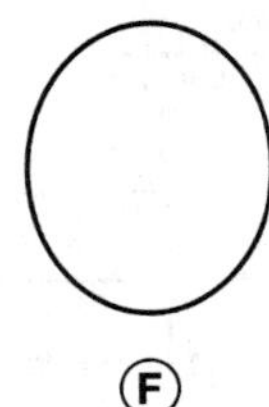
Ⓕ

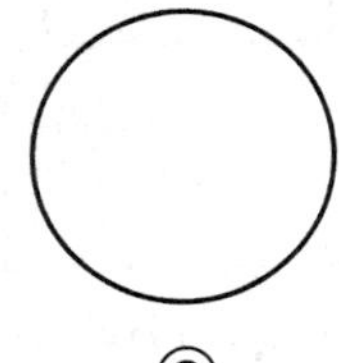
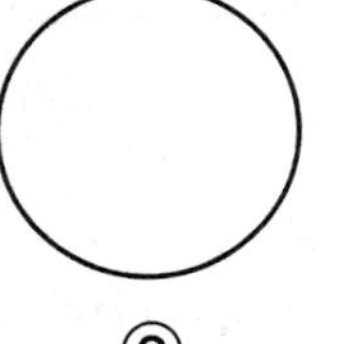
Ⓖ

Ⓗ

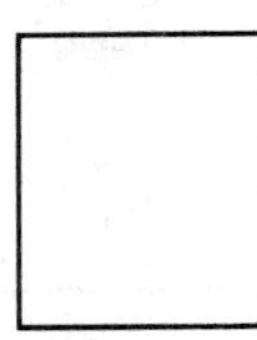
Ⓙ

---

7 What is the perimeter of the figure?

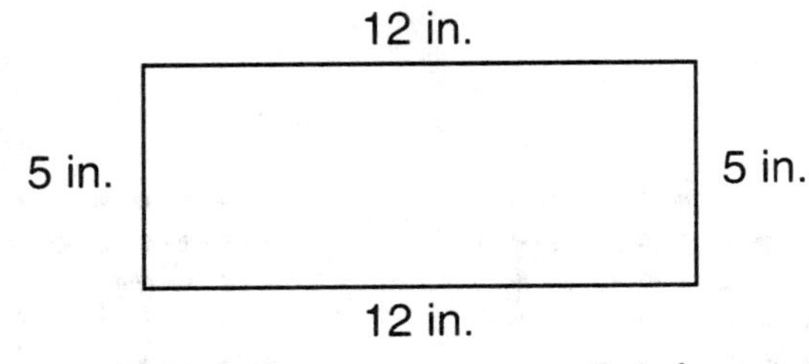

14 in.	29 in.	34 in.	10 in.
Ⓐ	Ⓑ	Ⓒ	Ⓓ

GO

8 Look at these pairs of shapes. Which one is a pair of triangles?

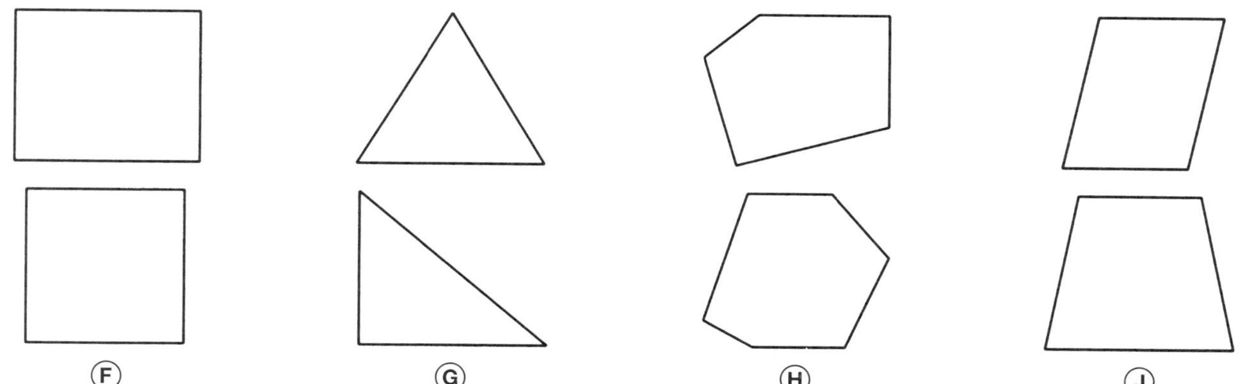

Ⓕ Ⓖ Ⓗ Ⓙ

9 Which figure's two sides will not match when the two sides are folded?

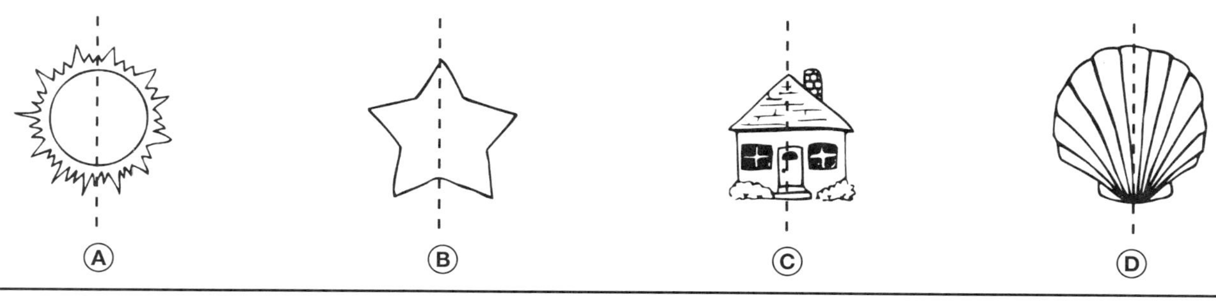

Ⓐ Ⓑ Ⓒ Ⓓ

10 What is the name of this figure?

sphere Ⓕ cylinder Ⓖ cube Ⓗ cone Ⓙ

11 What is the perimeter of this figure?

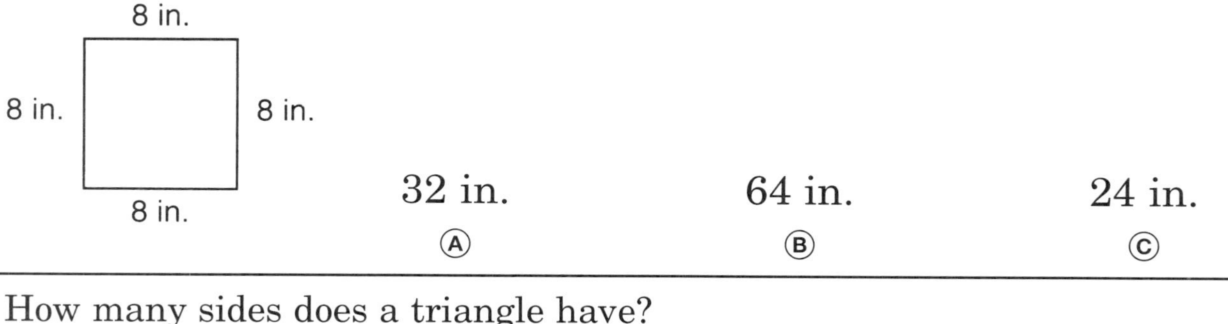

32 in. Ⓐ 64 in. Ⓑ 24 in. Ⓒ

12 How many sides does a triangle have?

3 Ⓕ 1 Ⓖ 4 Ⓗ 5 Ⓙ

STOP

Example **Directions:** Choose the best answer to the question.

A Practice on this one.

What time does the clock show?

10:35	7:10	2:35	7:02
Ⓐ	Ⓑ	Ⓒ	Ⓓ

If you work on scratch paper, be sure you copy numbers correctly and compute carefully.

Practice

1 Look at the objects. Which object might weigh about five pounds?

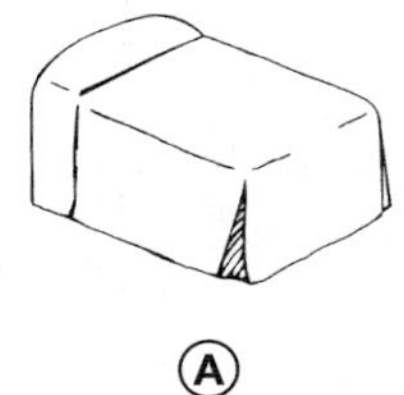
Ⓐ

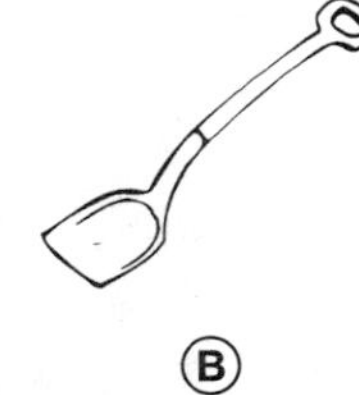
Ⓑ

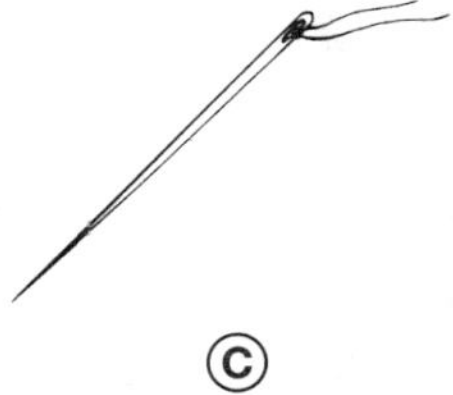
Ⓒ

Ⓓ

2 In which month is the 20th on Sunday?

SEPTEMBER

S	M	T	W	T	F	S
			1	2	3	4
5	6	7	8	9	10	11
12	13	14	15	16	17	18
19	20	21	22	23	24	25
26	27	28	29	30		

Ⓕ

OCTOBER

S	M	T	W	T	F	S
					1	2
3	4	5	6	7	8	9
10	11	12	13	14	15	16
17	18	19	20	21	22	23
24	25	26	27	28	29	30
31						

Ⓖ

NOVEMBER

S	M	T	W	T	F	S
		1	2	3	4	5
6	7	8	9	10	11	12
13	14	15	16	17	18	19
20	21	22	23	24	25	26
27	28	29	30			

Ⓗ

DECEMBER

S	M	T	W	T	F	S
				1	2	3
4	5	6	7	8	9	10
11	12	13	14	15	16	17
18	19	20	21	22	23	24
25	26	27	28	29	30	31

Ⓙ

3 Look at these coins. How much money do they show?

51¢	66¢	62¢	76¢
Ⓐ	Ⓑ	Ⓒ	Ⓓ

GO

4 Which number shows five dollars and ninety-three cents?

$5.93	$5.39	$593	$.593
Ⓕ	Ⓖ	Ⓗ	Ⓙ

---

5 Which metric unit would be best used to show how tall someone is?

liter	meter	kilogram	kilometer
Ⓐ	Ⓑ	Ⓒ	Ⓓ

---

6 Look at each clock. The first one shows what time the movie began. The second one shows what time it ended. How long was the movie?

15 minutes	11 hours	12 hours	2 hours
Ⓕ	Ⓖ	Ⓗ	Ⓙ

Look at this calendar.

MAY						
SUN	MON	TUE	WED	THU	FRI	SAT
	1	2	3	4	5	6
7	8	9	10	11	12	13
14	15	16	17	18	19	20
21	22	23	24	25	26	27
28	29	30	31			

---

7 What date is the second Thursday in May?

May 11	May 18	May 12	May 14
Ⓐ	Ⓑ	Ⓒ	Ⓓ

---

8 What day of the week is May 9?

Sunday	Wednesday	Tuesday	Friday
Ⓕ	Ⓖ	Ⓗ	Ⓙ

GO

Look at this picture.

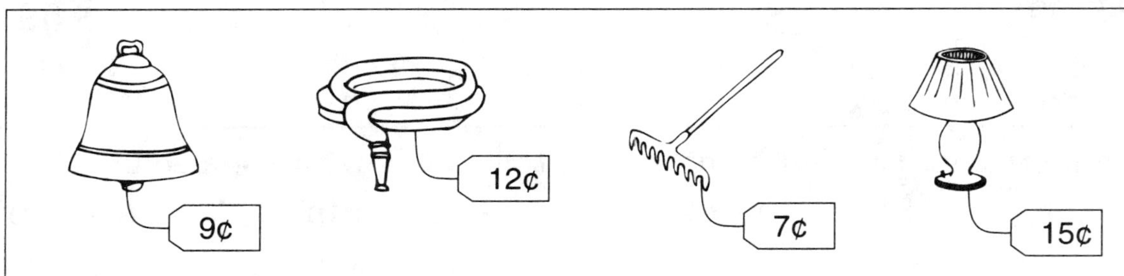

9 Which object costs the most?

   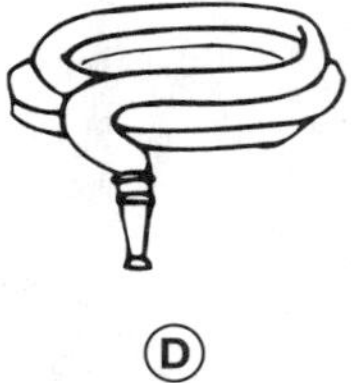

Ⓐ Ⓑ Ⓒ Ⓓ

10 Which object can you buy for a quarter and get exactly 18¢ in change?

  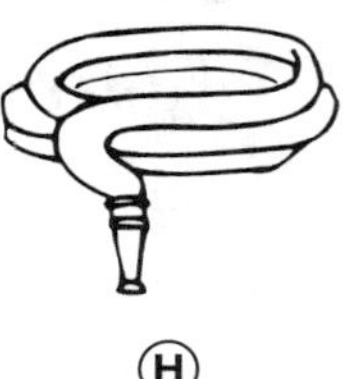 

Ⓕ Ⓖ Ⓗ Ⓙ

11 How much would it cost to buy a hose and a rake?

24¢	12¢	7¢	19¢
Ⓐ	Ⓑ	Ⓒ	Ⓓ

12 Look at the ruler and the lines. What is the difference in length between the lines?

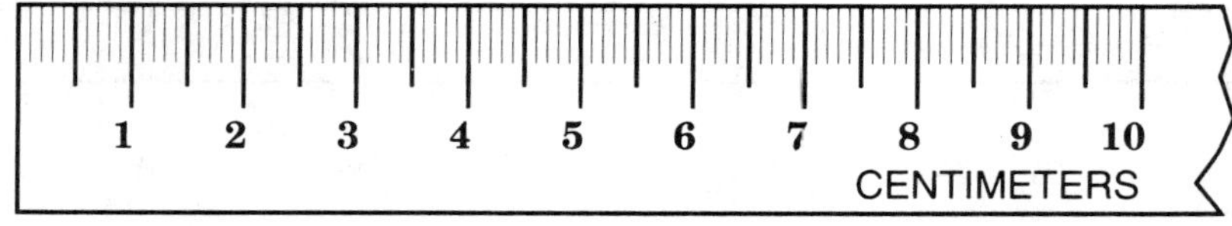

4 cm	13 cm	5 cm	9 cm
Ⓕ	Ⓖ	Ⓗ	Ⓙ

GO

13 Which thermometer shows the temperature on a hot summer day?

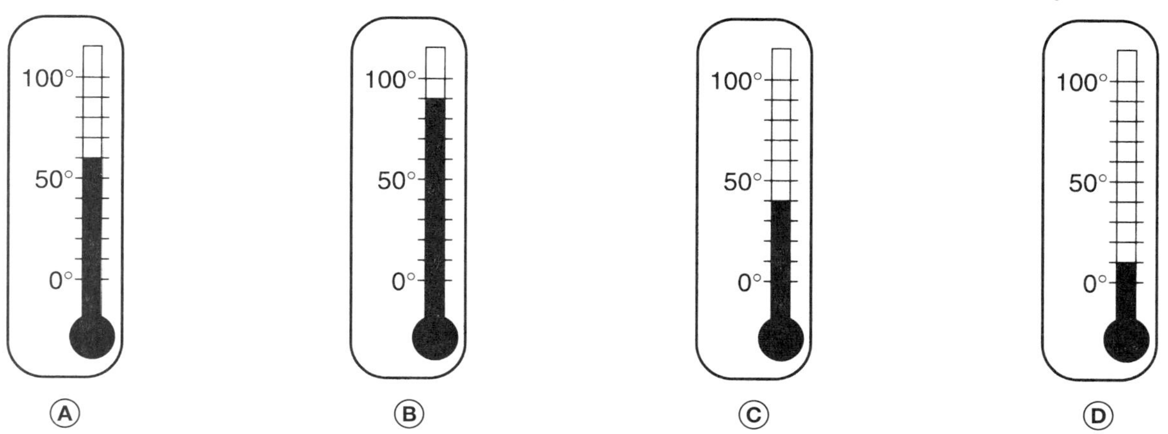

14 Look at the ovals and the ruler. How many of the ovals are more than three inches long?

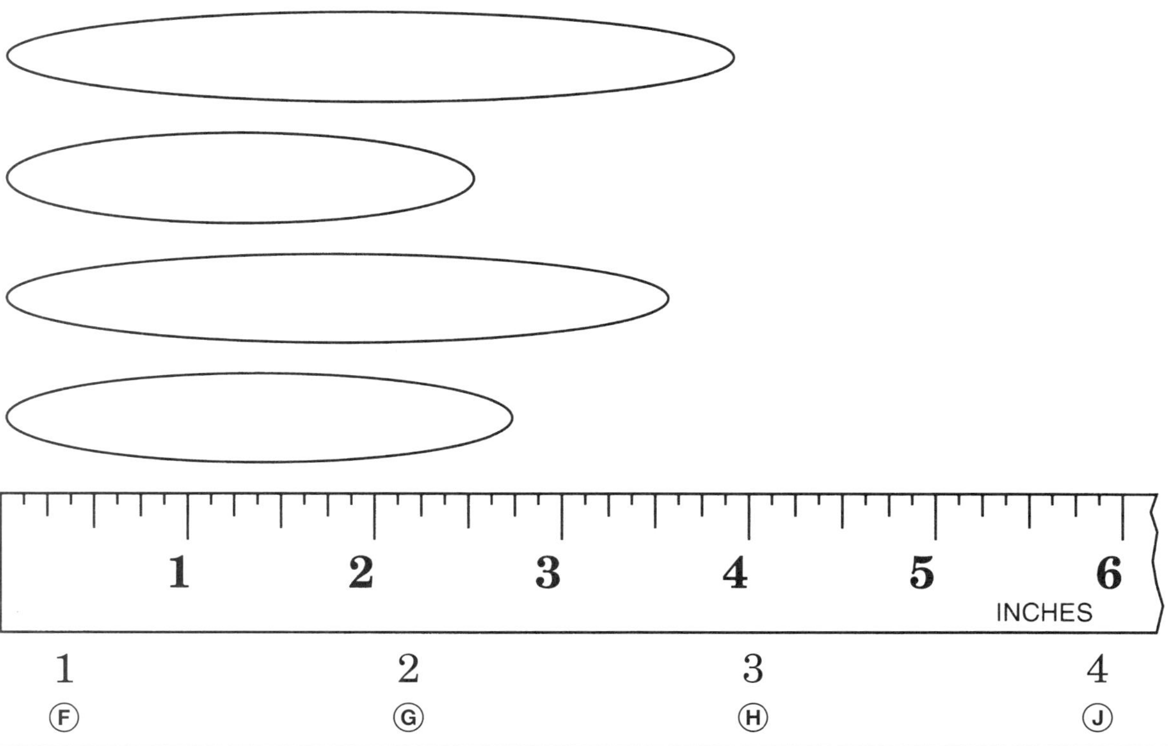

1 Ⓕ 2 Ⓖ 3 Ⓗ 4 Ⓙ

15 It started to snow at ten o'clock. It stopped twenty minutes later. What time was it when it stopped snowing?

GO

16 Which is another way to say fifteen minutes before noon?

12:15	11:15	11:45	12:45
Ⓕ	Ⓖ	Ⓗ	Ⓙ

---

17 Which one of these objects is about six inches long?

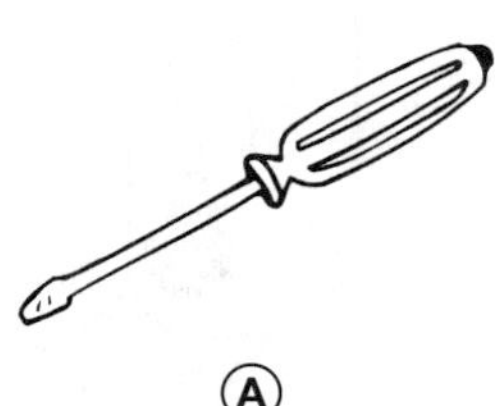

Ⓐ Ⓑ Ⓒ Ⓓ

---

18 Which number shows how many minutes there are in an hour?

30	60	15	12
Ⓕ	Ⓖ	Ⓗ	Ⓙ

---

19 The time the clock shows is fifteen minutes after what time?

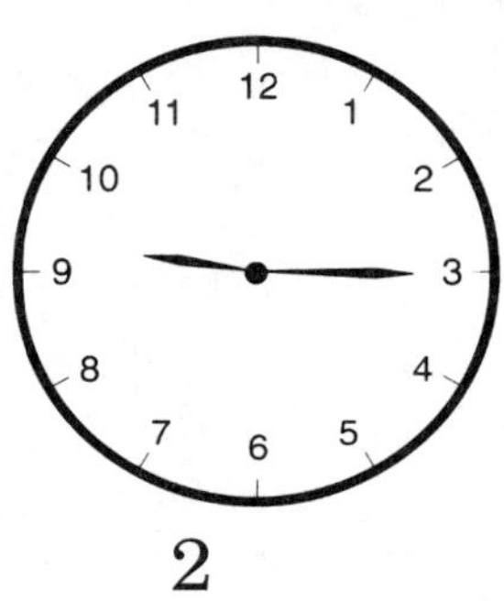

2	3	10	9
Ⓐ	Ⓑ	Ⓒ	Ⓓ

---

20 Pretend you had the money below. Then you found a dime. How much would you have?

75¢	65¢	70¢	60¢
Ⓕ	Ⓖ	Ⓗ	Ⓙ

---

21 How much change would you have if you bought something that cost a quarter and paid for it with half a dollar?

50¢	25¢	$1.00	75¢
Ⓐ	Ⓑ	Ⓒ	Ⓓ

STOP

Example **Directions:** Read or listen to the story. Then choose the best answer. If the answer is not shown, choose N.

A This one has been done for you.

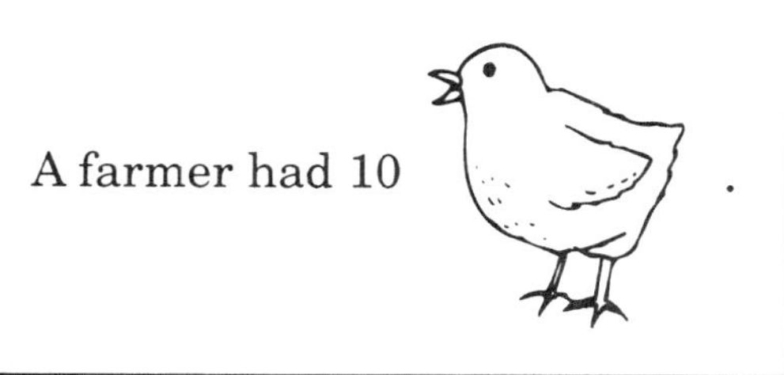

A farmer had 10 chicks. He gave 4 away. How many did he have?

40	5	6	N
Ⓐ	Ⓑ	●	Ⓓ

Do numbers 1-4 the same way.

Listen to the whole problem and think about what you should do before you choose an answer.

Practice

1 Twenty-three students went to the library. Ten of them used computers. The rest looked at books. How many looked at books?

13	35	12	N
Ⓐ	Ⓑ	Ⓒ	Ⓓ

2 Apples cost 15¢ a pound. Pears cost 5¢ a pound more. How much do pears cost?

10¢	25¢	20¢	N
Ⓕ	Ⓖ	Ⓗ	Ⓙ

3 A large school bus can carry 40 students. A small school bus can carry half as many. How many students can the small bus carry?

38	10	22	N
Ⓐ	Ⓑ	Ⓒ	Ⓓ

4 A boy washed 2 pans, 4 pots, and 8 plates. How many things did he wash?

16	14	12	N
Ⓕ	Ⓖ	Ⓗ	Ⓙ

GO

5 Look at the graph. How would you move from the circle to the square?

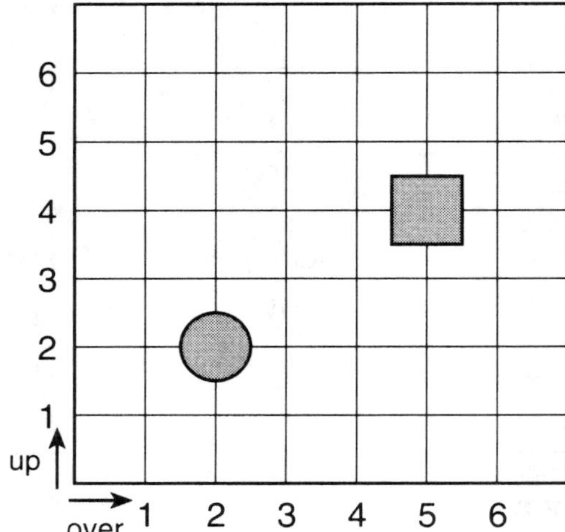

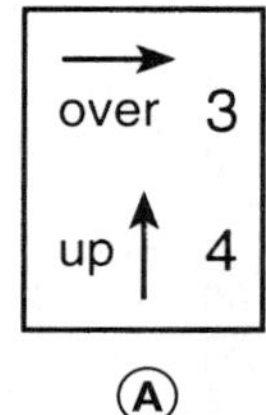

Ⓐ

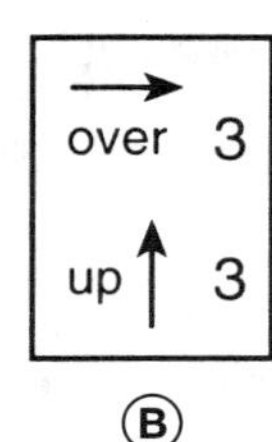

Ⓑ

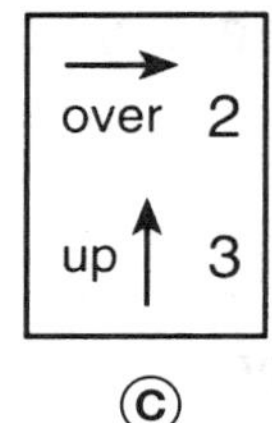

Ⓒ

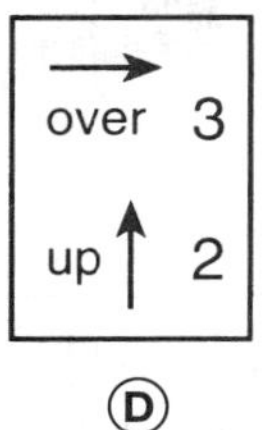

Ⓓ

6 One morning, there were 8 cars parked on a street. The owners drove 2 of the cars away. How many cars were left on the street?

10	2	6	N
Ⓕ	Ⓖ	Ⓗ	Ⓙ

7 Maureen earned \$12 working for her uncle. She already had \$5. How much money did she have all together?

\$17	\$7	\$18	N
Ⓐ	Ⓑ	Ⓒ	Ⓓ

8 The packages that Jonas mailed weighed 2 pounds, 5 pounds, and 8 pounds. How much did the packages weigh all together?

Ⓕ $8 - 5 - 2 =$

Ⓖ $8 + 5 + 2 =$

Ⓗ $8 \times 5 \times 2 =$

9 Ruby is 14 years old. Her brother is 8 years younger. How can you find out how old her brother is?

Ⓐ Subtract 14 from 8.

Ⓑ Add 14 and 8.

Ⓒ Subtract 8 from 14.

GO

Look at the different bones in the box.

10 Which color of bone has the largest amount?

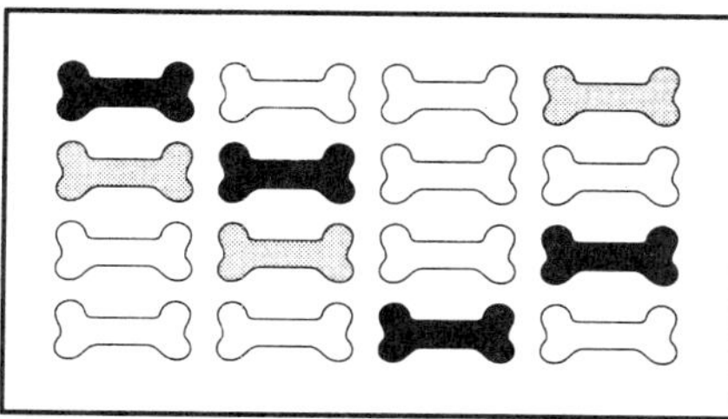

Look at the graph. Then answer questions 11-14.

Parks and Schools in Five Cities

	CITY 1	CITY 2	CITY 3	CITY 4	CITY 5
Number of Parks	8	16	2	9	4
Number of Schools	7	12	5	6	4

11 How many parks does City 4 have?

6 (A)   9 (B)   2 (C)   4 (D)

12 Which city has the fewest schools?

City 5 (F)   City 3 (G)   City 1 (H)   City 4 (J)

13 Which city has the most parks and schools all together?

City 3 (A)   City 1 (B)   City 5 (C)   City 2 (D)

14 How many more parks than schools does City 4 have?

15 (F)   2 (G)   3 (H)   4 (J)

GO

Directions: Choose the number sentence that shows how to solve the problem or solve the problem to find the right answer.

15 A clown is holding 8 red balloons and 9 blue balloons. How many balloons is the clown holding in all?

Ⓐ $9 - 8 = \square$

Ⓑ $8 \times 9 = \square$

Ⓒ $8 + 9 = \square$

Ⓓ $9 \div 8 = \square$

16 Chico runs 3 miles a day 5 days a week. How far does he run in a week?

Ⓕ $5 \times 3 = \square$

Ⓖ $5 - 3 = \square$

Ⓗ $3 + 5 = \square$

Ⓙ $3 \div 5 = \square$

17 There are 100 nails in a box. Diana used 12 of them. How many are left?

Ⓐ $25 \times 100 = \square$

Ⓑ $100 - 25 = \square$

Ⓒ $25 + 100 = \square$

Ⓓ $100 \div 25 = \square$

18 A candy bar costs 15¢. How much change will you receive if you pay for the candy bar with two dimes?

Ⓕ 30¢

Ⓖ 10¢

Ⓗ 35¢

Ⓙ 5¢

19 A tree is 18 inches tall. How tall would it be if it grew 6 more inches?

Ⓐ 12 inches

Ⓑ 24 inches

Ⓒ 26 inches

Ⓓ 30 inches

20 In the morning, there were 35 boxes of cereal on a store shelf. At the end of the day, there were only 7 boxes left. How many boxes of cereal were sold that day?

Ⓕ $35 - \square = 7$

Ⓖ $\square - 7 = 35$

Ⓗ $7 + 35 = \square$

Ⓙ $\square - 35 = 7$

21 Sandy found that there are 4 quarts of water in a bucket. How many quarts of water are in 5 buckets?

Ⓐ $5 - 4 = \square$

Ⓑ $5 \div 4 = \square$

Ⓒ $5 \times 4 = \square$

Ⓓ $5 + 4 = \square$

22 Max has 38 bottles to recycle. Susan has 42 bottles to recycle. How many bottles in all do they have to recycle?

Ⓕ 70

Ⓖ 4

Ⓗ 75

Ⓙ 80

STOP

Directions: Read or listen to the question. Choose the best answer.

This one has been done for you. Do numbers 1-20 the same way.

E1 Look at this folded piece of paper. A piece has been cut out of it and then unfolded. Which answer matches that unfolded shape?

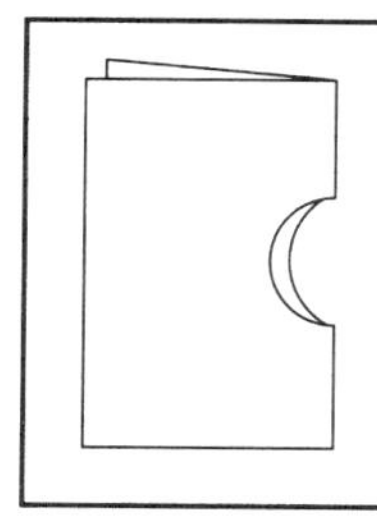

Ⓐ

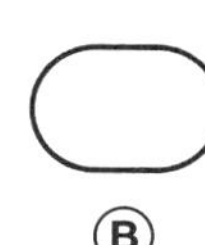
Ⓑ

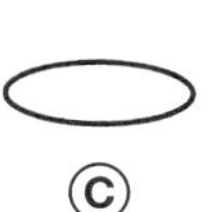
Ⓒ

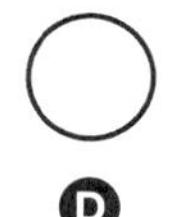
● D

1 How many of these shapes have more than three sides?

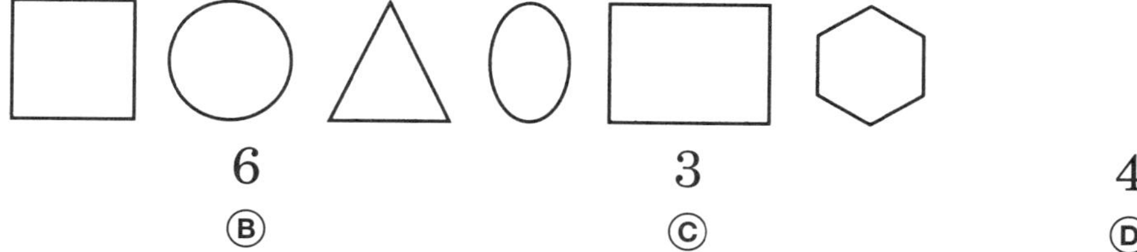

0	6	3	4
Ⓐ	Ⓑ	Ⓒ	Ⓓ

2 Which clock reads 12:15?

Ⓕ

Ⓖ

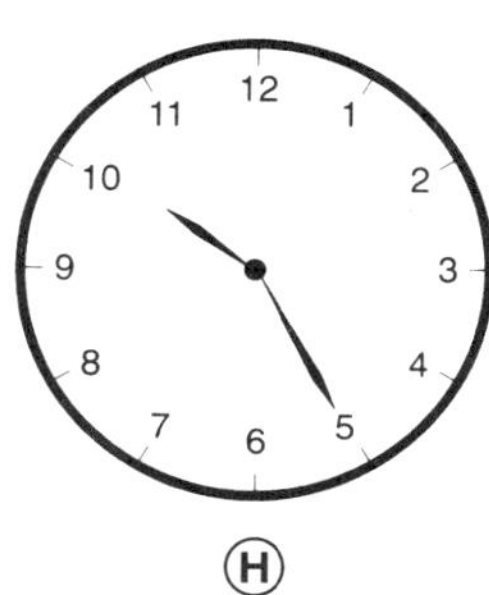
Ⓗ

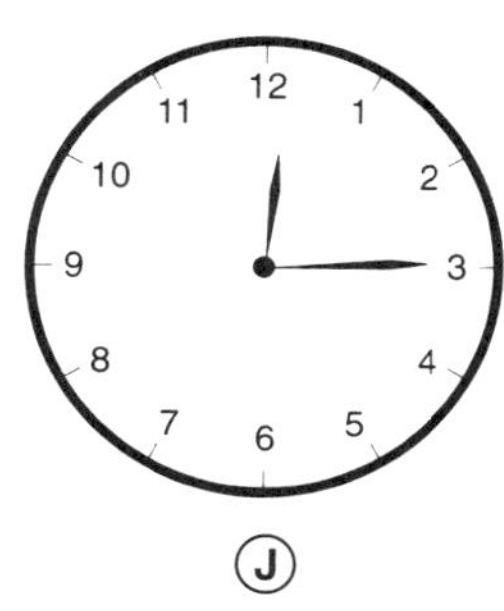
Ⓙ

3 Which figure matches the one in the box?

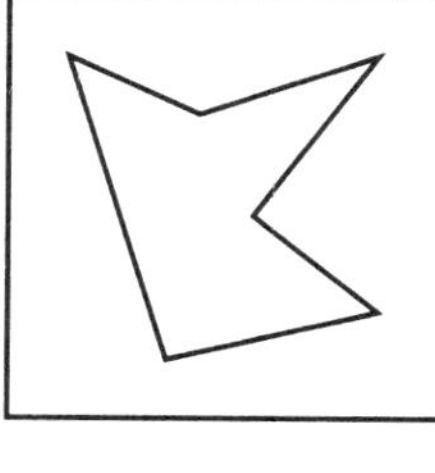

Ⓐ

Ⓑ

Ⓒ

Ⓓ

4 How many more black circles are there than white circles?

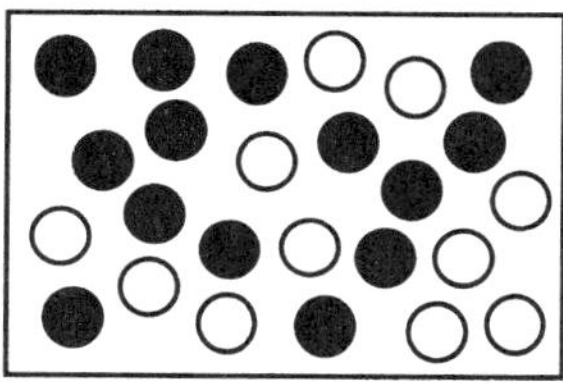

11	3	14	4
Ⓕ	Ⓖ	Ⓗ	Ⓙ

GO

5 Look at the calendar. October comes after September. What day of the week is October 1?

SEPTEMBER						
S	M	T	W	T	F	S
			1	2	3	4
5	6	7	8	9	10	11
12	13	14	15	16	17	18
19	20	21	22	23	24	25
26	27	28	29	30		

Wednesday Ⓐ   Saturday Ⓑ   Monday Ⓒ   Friday Ⓓ

Look at this graph. Then answer questions 6-8.

Monday	🦭 🦭
Tuesday	🦭 🦭 🦭 🦭
Wednesday	🦭 🦭 🦭
Thursday	🦭 🦭 🦭 🦭 🦭
Friday	🦭 🦭

6 On which days of the week were two seals seen?

Monday and Friday Ⓕ   Monday and Thursday Ⓖ   Friday and Wednesday Ⓗ   Friday and Tuesday Ⓙ

7 How many more seals were seen on Thursday than Friday?

1 Ⓐ   4 Ⓑ   3 Ⓒ   2 Ⓓ

8 How many more seals were seen all together on Monday, Tuesday, and Wednesday?

10 Ⓕ   9 Ⓖ   8 Ⓗ   12 Ⓙ

GO

9 A can of tennis balls holds three balls. How many balls are in 5 cans? Pick the right number sentence.

Ⓐ $5 \div 3 = \square$
Ⓑ $3 \times 5 = \square$
Ⓒ $5 - 3 = \square$
Ⓓ $3 + 5 = \square$

10 Mrs. James bought 2 loaves of bread, 5 bottles of juice, and three cans of soup. How many things did she buy? Choose the right number sentence.

Ⓕ $2 - 5 - 3 = \square$
Ⓖ $2 \times 5 + 3 = \square$
Ⓗ $2 \div 5 + 3 = \square$
Ⓙ $2 + 5 + 3 = \square$

11 There are 33 people on a plane. When it lands, 17 of the people get off. The rest stay on the plane and fly to the next city. How many people stayed on the plane?

Ⓐ 50
Ⓑ 12
Ⓒ 17
Ⓓ N

12 What is the perimeter of the figure?

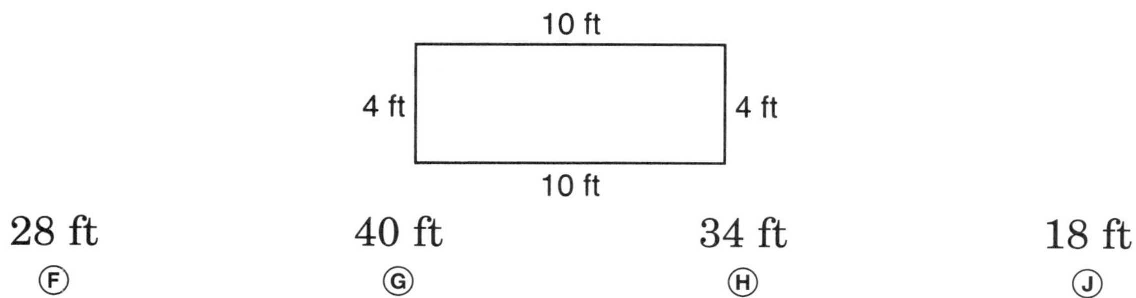

28 ft	40 ft	34 ft	18 ft
Ⓕ	Ⓖ	Ⓗ	Ⓙ

13 The first clock shows the time that Maggie started studying. The second clock shows when she finished. How long did she study?

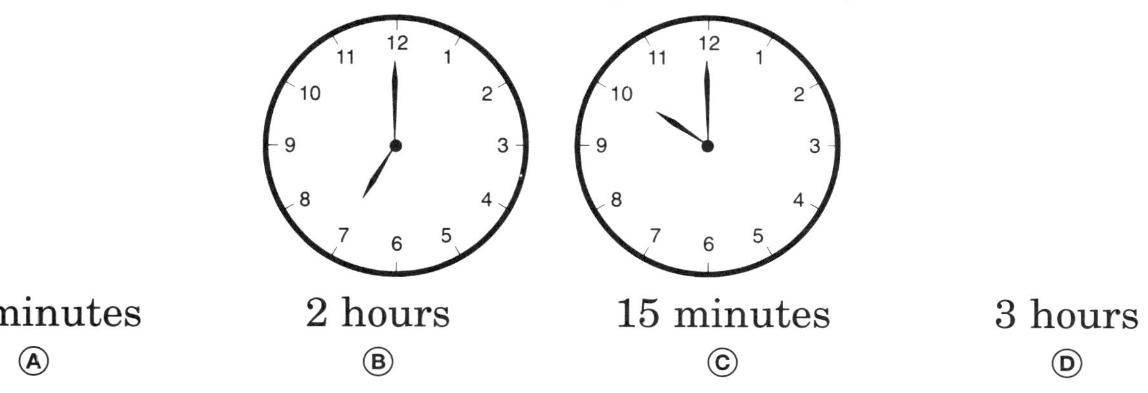

50 minutes	2 hours	15 minutes	3 hours
Ⓐ	Ⓑ	Ⓒ	Ⓓ

GO

14 Noah had 21 baseball cards. He bought 8 more. How many did he have in all? Choose the right number sentence.

Ⓕ $8 - 21 = \square$
Ⓖ $8 \times 21 = \square$
Ⓗ $21 + 8 = \square$
Ⓙ $21 \div 8 = \square$

15 A car is traveling 45 miles an hour. It slows to 25 miles an hour. Which number sentence shows how much slower the car is going?

Ⓐ $45 - \square = 25$
Ⓑ $45 + \square = 25$
Ⓒ $25 - \square = 45$
Ⓓ $25 + 45 = \square$

16 A toy costs 39¢. If you paid for the toy with 50¢, how much change would you get back?

Ⓕ 24¢
Ⓖ 89¢
Ⓗ 21¢
Ⓙ 11¢

17 Frank has 24 feet of wire. He uses 15 feet of wire to repair a fence. How many feet of wire does Frank have left?

Ⓐ $24 - 15 = \square$
Ⓑ $\square - 15 = 24$
Ⓒ $24 + 12 = \square$
Ⓓ $\square - 24 = 15$

18 The students in a class are divided into 4 teams of 6 students each. How many students are in the class?

Ⓕ $6 - \square = 4$
Ⓖ $\square - 6 = 4$
Ⓗ $4 \times 6 = \square$
Ⓙ $\square + 4 = 6$

19 In May, Amanda mowed the lawn 6 times. In June, she mowed it 5 times, and in July, only 2 times. How many times in all did Amanda mow the lawn in May, June, and July?

Ⓐ 11
Ⓑ 13
Ⓒ 14
Ⓓ 10

20 A building in a city has 39 floors. People live on 27 floors of the building and the other floors are used for stores. How many floors are used for stores?

Ⓕ 22
Ⓖ 12
Ⓗ 66
Ⓙ 14

STOP

NUMBER RIGHT ______

Name and Answer Sheet

To the Student:

These tests will give you a chance to put the tips you have learned to work.

A few last reminders . . .

- Be sure you understand all the directions before you begin each test. You may ask the teacher questions about the directions if you do not understand them.
- Work as quickly as you can during each test.
- When you change an answer, be sure to erase your first mark completely.
- You can guess at an answer or skip difficult items and go back to them later.
- Use the tips you have learned whenever you can.
- It is OK to be a little nervous. You may even do better.

Now that you have completed the lessons in this unit, you are on your way to scoring high!

STUDENT'S NAME

LAST | FIRST | MI

A B C D E F G H I J K L M N O P Q R S T U V W X Y Z

SCHOOL

TEACHER

FEMALE ◯ MALE ◯

BIRTHDATE

MONTH	DAY		YEAR	
JAN	0	0		0
FEB	1	1		1
MAR	2	2		2
APR	3	3		3
MAY		4		4
JUN		5	5	5
JUL		6	6	6
AUG		7	7	7
SEP		8	8	8
OCT		9	9	9
NOV				
DEC				

GRADE

1 2 3

PART 1 CONCEPTS

E1 Ⓐ Ⓑ Ⓒ Ⓓ	4 Ⓕ Ⓖ Ⓗ Ⓙ	8 Ⓕ Ⓖ Ⓗ Ⓙ	12 Ⓕ Ⓖ Ⓗ Ⓙ	16 Ⓕ Ⓖ Ⓗ Ⓙ
1 Ⓐ Ⓑ Ⓒ Ⓓ	5 Ⓐ Ⓑ Ⓒ Ⓓ	9 Ⓐ Ⓑ Ⓒ Ⓓ	13 Ⓐ Ⓑ Ⓒ Ⓓ	17 Ⓐ Ⓑ Ⓒ Ⓓ
2 Ⓕ Ⓖ Ⓗ Ⓙ	6 Ⓕ Ⓖ Ⓗ Ⓙ	10 Ⓕ Ⓖ Ⓗ Ⓙ	14 Ⓕ Ⓖ Ⓗ Ⓙ	18 Ⓕ Ⓖ Ⓗ Ⓙ
3 Ⓐ Ⓑ Ⓒ Ⓓ	7 Ⓐ Ⓑ Ⓒ Ⓓ	11 Ⓐ Ⓑ Ⓒ Ⓓ	15 Ⓐ Ⓑ Ⓒ Ⓓ	19 Ⓐ Ⓑ Ⓒ Ⓓ

PART 2 COMPUTATION

E1 Ⓐ Ⓑ Ⓒ Ⓓ Ⓔ	3 Ⓐ Ⓑ Ⓒ Ⓓ Ⓔ	7 Ⓐ Ⓑ Ⓒ Ⓓ Ⓔ	11 Ⓐ Ⓑ Ⓒ Ⓓ Ⓔ	15 Ⓐ Ⓑ Ⓒ Ⓓ Ⓔ
E2 Ⓕ Ⓖ Ⓗ Ⓙ Ⓚ	4 Ⓕ Ⓖ Ⓗ Ⓙ Ⓚ	8 Ⓕ Ⓖ Ⓗ Ⓙ Ⓚ	12 Ⓕ Ⓖ Ⓗ Ⓙ Ⓚ	16 Ⓕ Ⓖ Ⓗ Ⓙ Ⓚ
1 Ⓐ Ⓑ Ⓒ Ⓓ Ⓔ	5 Ⓐ Ⓑ Ⓒ Ⓓ Ⓔ	9 Ⓐ Ⓑ Ⓒ Ⓓ Ⓔ	13 Ⓐ Ⓑ Ⓒ Ⓓ Ⓔ	17 Ⓐ Ⓑ Ⓒ Ⓓ Ⓔ
2 Ⓕ Ⓖ Ⓗ Ⓙ Ⓚ	6 Ⓕ Ⓖ Ⓗ Ⓙ Ⓚ	10 Ⓕ Ⓖ Ⓗ Ⓙ Ⓚ	14 Ⓕ Ⓖ Ⓗ Ⓙ Ⓚ	18 Ⓕ Ⓖ Ⓗ Ⓙ Ⓚ

PART 3 APPLICATIONS

E1 Ⓐ Ⓑ Ⓒ Ⓓ	5 Ⓐ Ⓑ Ⓒ Ⓓ	10 Ⓕ Ⓖ Ⓗ Ⓙ	15 Ⓐ Ⓑ Ⓒ Ⓓ	20 Ⓕ Ⓖ Ⓗ Ⓙ
1 Ⓐ Ⓑ Ⓒ Ⓓ	6 Ⓕ Ⓖ Ⓗ Ⓙ	11 Ⓐ Ⓑ Ⓒ Ⓓ	16 Ⓕ Ⓖ Ⓗ Ⓙ	21 Ⓐ Ⓑ Ⓒ Ⓓ
2 Ⓕ Ⓖ Ⓗ Ⓙ	7 Ⓐ Ⓑ Ⓒ Ⓓ	12 Ⓕ Ⓖ Ⓗ Ⓙ	17 Ⓐ Ⓑ Ⓒ Ⓓ	
3 Ⓐ Ⓑ Ⓒ Ⓓ	8 Ⓕ Ⓖ Ⓗ Ⓙ	13 Ⓐ Ⓑ Ⓒ Ⓓ	18 Ⓕ Ⓖ Ⓗ Ⓙ	
4 Ⓕ Ⓖ Ⓗ Ⓙ	9 Ⓐ Ⓑ Ⓒ Ⓓ	14 Ⓕ Ⓖ Ⓗ Ⓙ	19 Ⓐ Ⓑ Ⓒ Ⓓ	

Part 1 Concepts

Directions: Listen to or read each question. Choose the best answer.

This one has been done for you.

E1 Which one shows the expanded numeral for two hundred fifty-seven?

200 + 150 + 57	200 + 70 + 5	200 + 50 + 7	2 + 100 + 50 + 7
Ⓐ	Ⓑ	●	Ⓓ

1 Look at the number line. Which numeral should replace the circle?

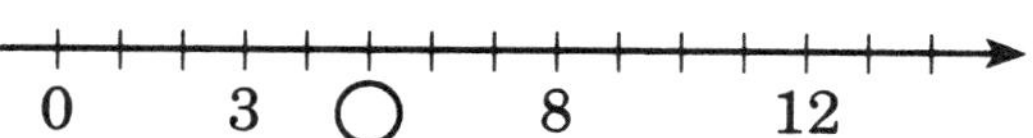

5	4	7	6
Ⓐ	Ⓑ	Ⓒ	Ⓓ

2 Look at the hundreds, tens, and ones chart. What number is shown on the chart?

100s	10s	1
● ● ● ● ● ● ● ●		● ● ● ● ●

801	85	850	805
Ⓕ	Ⓖ	Ⓗ	Ⓙ

3 Which square is seventh from the circle?

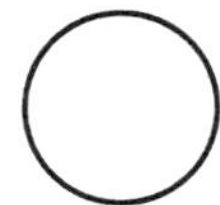 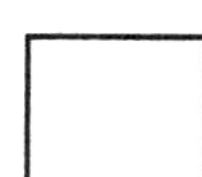     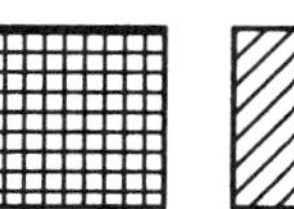 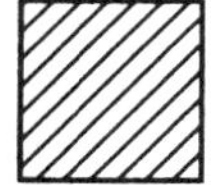

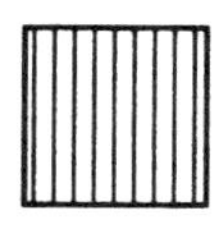		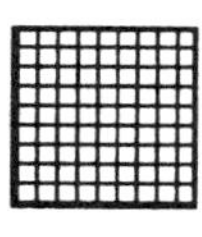	
Ⓐ	Ⓑ	Ⓒ	Ⓓ

4 Which numbers go in the blank spaces when you count by ones?

78, ____ , 80, 81, ____ , 83

77, 82	79, 84	78, 84	79, 82
Ⓕ	Ⓖ	Ⓗ	Ⓙ

GO

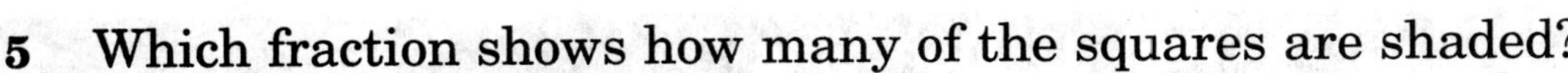

5 Which fraction shows how many of the squares are shaded?

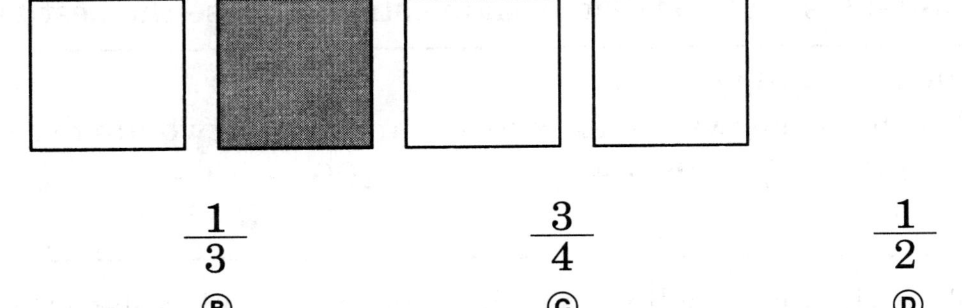

$\frac{1}{4}$ Ⓐ　　$\frac{1}{3}$ Ⓑ　　$\frac{3}{4}$ Ⓒ　　$\frac{1}{2}$ Ⓓ

---

6 Which number is five hundred sixty-one?

516 Ⓕ　　5601 Ⓖ　　561 Ⓗ　　50,061 Ⓙ

---

7 Look at the pattern. Which part of the pattern comes next?

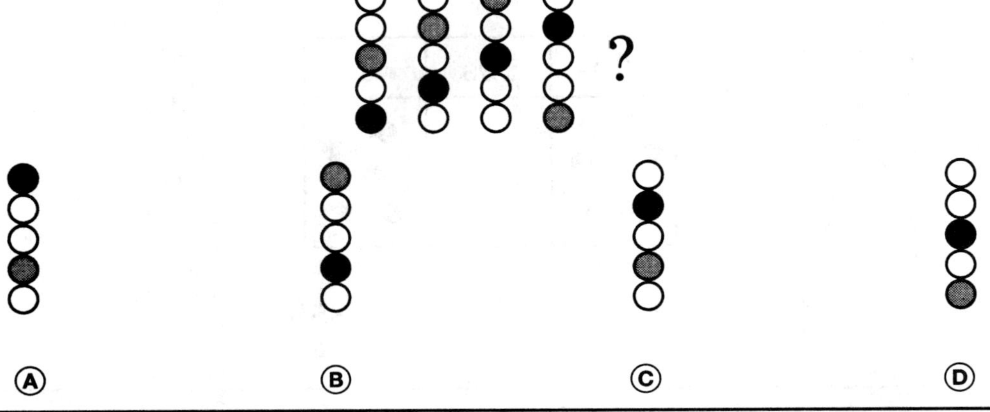

Ⓐ　　Ⓑ　　Ⓒ　　Ⓓ

---

8 Which number should go in the boxes to make both number sentences true?

$$12 + \square = 28$$
$$24 - \square = 8$$

15 Ⓕ　　14 Ⓖ　　12 Ⓗ　　16 Ⓙ

---

9 What is another way to write 29 is greater than 22?

$29 = 22$ Ⓐ　　$22 < 29$ Ⓑ　　$22 > 29$ Ⓒ　　$29 < 22$ Ⓓ

GO

10 Look at the squares in the box. How many are there total?

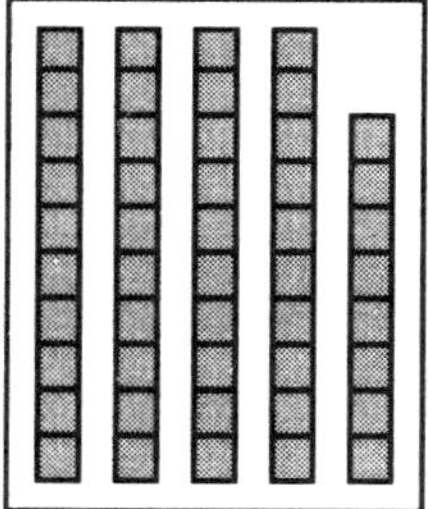

58	48	52	50
Ⓕ	Ⓖ	Ⓗ	Ⓙ

11 Which symbol goes in the number sentence to make it true?

$32 \bigcirc 27 = 5$

+	−	×	÷
Ⓐ	Ⓑ	Ⓒ	Ⓓ

12 Look at the number table. The "in" numbers are changed in some way to different numbers when they come "out." How have they been changed?

IN	OUT
20	13
23	16
29	22

subtract 7	add 7	add 6	subtract 6
Ⓕ	Ⓖ	Ⓗ	Ⓙ

13 Which number is between 36 and 45?

28	47	35	39
Ⓐ	Ⓑ	Ⓒ	Ⓓ

14 Which number is missing from this number sequence?

27, 32, ____, 42, 47

33	39	37	35
Ⓕ	Ⓖ	Ⓗ	Ⓙ

GO

15 How many of these problems have an answer of nine?

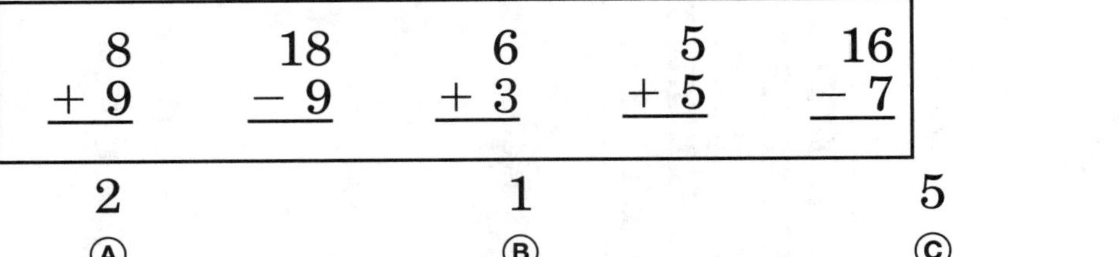

2 Ⓐ 1 Ⓑ 5 Ⓒ 3 Ⓓ

---

16 Which number word fits in the blank to complete the pattern?

eighteen, nineteen, ____________, twenty-one

seventeen Ⓕ twenty Ⓖ twenty-one Ⓗ nineteen Ⓙ

---

17 How many dots are there in all?

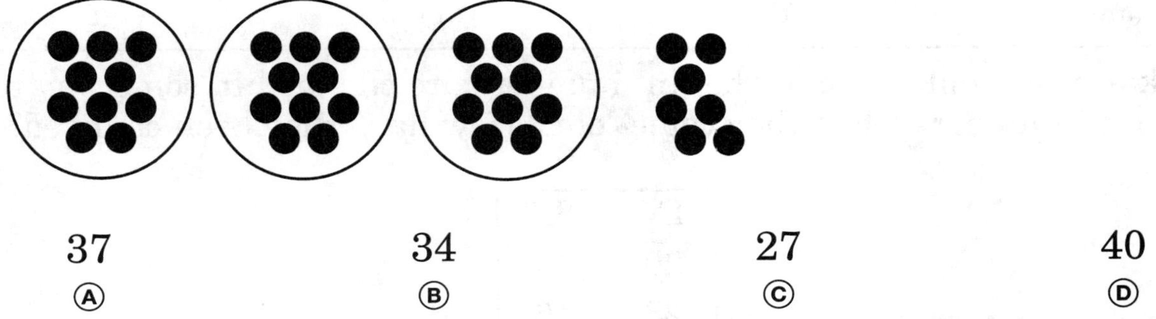

37 Ⓐ 34 Ⓑ 27 Ⓒ 40 Ⓓ

---

18 Which number matches the number word in the box?

four thousand, two hundred and ten

420,010 Ⓕ 40,210 Ⓖ 4210 Ⓗ 4,002,010 Ⓙ

---

19 Which multiplication fact is shown by the dots in the box?

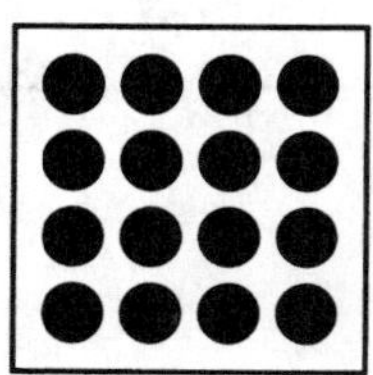

$2 \times 4 = 8$ Ⓐ $4 \times 4 = 16$ Ⓑ $3 \times 5 = 15$ Ⓒ $3 \times 4 = 12$ Ⓓ

STOP

Part 2 Computation

Directions: Read or listen to each problem. Choose the answer that is correct. Choose N if the answer is not shown.

E1 This one has been done for you.

$2 + 4 = \square$

2	3	7	N
Ⓐ	Ⓑ	Ⓒ	●

E2 Practice on this one.

$$\begin{array}{r} 6 \\ -\ 3 \\ \hline \end{array}$$

3 Ⓕ
9 Ⓖ
5 Ⓗ
18 Ⓙ

Do numbers 1-18 the same way.

1 $7 + 2 = \square$

5	11	9	N
Ⓐ	Ⓑ	Ⓒ	Ⓓ

2 $8 + 11 = \square$

19	3	17	N
Ⓕ	Ⓖ	Ⓗ	Ⓙ

3 $4 + 23 = \square$

27	19	63	N
Ⓐ	Ⓑ	Ⓒ	Ⓓ

4 $15 - 8 = \square$

9	23	8	N
Ⓕ	Ⓖ	Ⓗ	Ⓙ

5 $9 - 4 = \square$

15	5	12	N
Ⓐ	Ⓑ	Ⓒ	Ⓓ

6 $27 - 13 = \square$

40	16	14	N
Ⓕ	Ⓖ	Ⓗ	Ⓙ

7

$$\begin{array}{r} 300 \\ -\ 40 \\ \hline \end{array}$$

360 Ⓐ
260 Ⓑ
100 Ⓒ
340 Ⓓ

8

$98 + 21 = \square$

119 Ⓕ
100 Ⓖ
77 Ⓗ
129 Ⓙ

9

$$\begin{array}{r} 11 \\ 8 \\ +\ 6 \\ \hline \end{array}$$

52 Ⓐ
19 Ⓑ
35 Ⓒ
25 Ⓓ

10

$579 - 31 = \square$

448 Ⓕ
462 Ⓖ
548 Ⓗ
584 Ⓙ

GO

11

$$\begin{array}{r} 42¢ \\ -17¢ \\ \hline \end{array}$$

25 Ⓐ
35 Ⓑ
27 Ⓒ
31 Ⓓ

12

$4 + 5 + 2 + 9 = \square$

11 Ⓕ
22 Ⓖ
18 Ⓗ
20 Ⓙ

13

$$\begin{array}{r} 538 \\ -\ 269 \\ \hline \end{array}$$

261 Ⓐ
369 Ⓑ
269 Ⓒ
331 Ⓓ

14

$$\begin{array}{r} 37 \\ 21 \\ +\ 73 \\ \hline \end{array}$$

121 Ⓕ
94 Ⓖ
131 Ⓗ
58 Ⓙ

15

$$\begin{array}{r} 2 \\ \times\ 9 \\ \hline \end{array}$$

11 Ⓐ
28 Ⓑ
29 Ⓒ
18 Ⓓ

16

$8 \times 4 = \square$

32 Ⓕ
12 Ⓖ
48 Ⓗ
2 Ⓙ

17

$5 \overline{)25}$

30 Ⓐ
5 Ⓑ
20 Ⓒ
6 Ⓓ

18

$36 \div 9 = \square$

24 Ⓕ
4 Ⓖ
3 Ⓗ
12 Ⓙ

STOP

Directions: Read or listen to the question. Choose the correct answer.

E1 Look at the calendar. What is the date of the second Sunday in December?

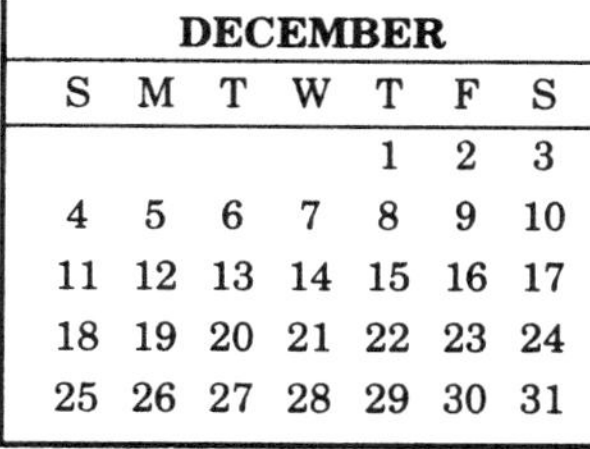

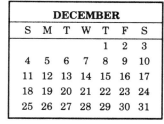

DECEMBER						
S	M	T	W	T	F	S
				1	2	3
4	5	6	7	8	9	10
11	12	13	14	15	16	17
18	19	20	21	22	23	24
25	26	27	28	29	30	31

Dec. 10 Ⓐ Dec. 2 Ⓑ Dec. 11 Ⓒ Dec. 4 Ⓓ

1 What is the perimeter of the figure?

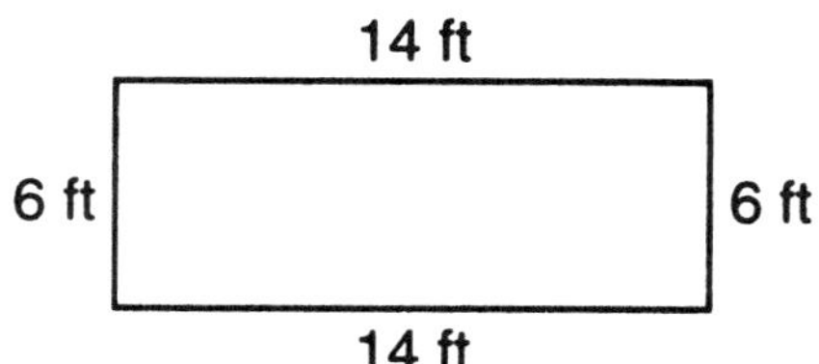

40 ft Ⓐ 28 ft Ⓑ 34 ft Ⓒ 36 ft Ⓓ

2 A case of fruit has 24 jars. How many jars are in two cases?

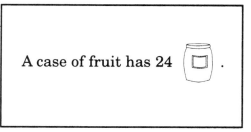

A case of fruit has 24 .

22 jars Ⓕ 26 jars Ⓖ 48 jars Ⓗ 50 jars Ⓙ

3 June lives halfway between the school and the lake. School is 18 miles from the lake. How many miles does June travel to school?

36 miles Ⓐ 8 miles Ⓑ 16 miles Ⓒ N Ⓓ

4 Carl read 8 books, Sandra read 10, Marty read 15. How many did they read all together?

23 Ⓕ 33 Ⓖ 35 Ⓗ N Ⓙ

GO

5 Which clock shows the time that is almost 10:30?

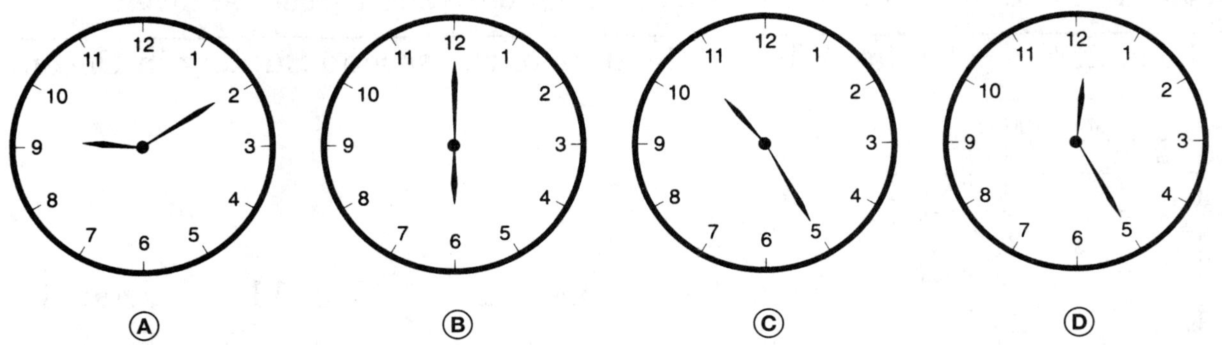

Look at this chart. Then answer questions 6-8.

Store 1	89¢	29¢	69¢
Store 2	79¢	25¢	69¢
Store 3	84¢	25¢	49¢
Store 4	89¢	25¢	57¢
Store 5	71¢	19¢	47¢

6 Which store has the lowest prices for all three things?

Store 4 Ⓕ   Store 1 Ⓖ   Store 3 Ⓗ   Store 5 Ⓙ

7 What is the most common price for pencils?

25¢ Ⓐ   29¢ Ⓑ   19¢ Ⓒ   69¢ Ⓓ

8 How much would you save if you bought crayons at Store 5 rather than Store 1?

71¢ Ⓕ   18¢ Ⓖ   19¢ Ⓗ   8¢ Ⓙ

GO

9 There are 7 days in a week. How many days are there in 4 weeks? Choose the right number sentence.

Ⓐ $7 \times 4 = \square$

Ⓑ $7 \div 4 = \square$

Ⓒ $7 - 4 = \square$

Ⓓ $7 + 4 = \square$

10 There are 32 ounces in one can of pizza sauce. Billy's mom used 8 ounces to make a pizza. How much sauce is left? Choose the right number sentence.

Ⓕ $32 \div 8 = \square$

Ⓖ $\square - 32 = 8$

Ⓗ $32 - \square = 8$

Ⓙ $32 + 8 = \square$

11 A team of 4 students each ran a race of 100 meters. Their times were 14 seconds, 15 seconds, 14 seconds, and 16 seconds. How long did it take the team to finish the race?

Ⓐ 59 seconds

Ⓑ 45 seconds

Ⓒ 69 seconds

Ⓓ N

12 Pretend you have a dollar to buy a sandwich. This is the change you received. How much did the sandwich cost?

63¢	59¢	47¢	53¢
Ⓕ	Ⓖ	Ⓗ	Ⓙ

13 Which of these triangles can be folded in half so that the parts match exactly?

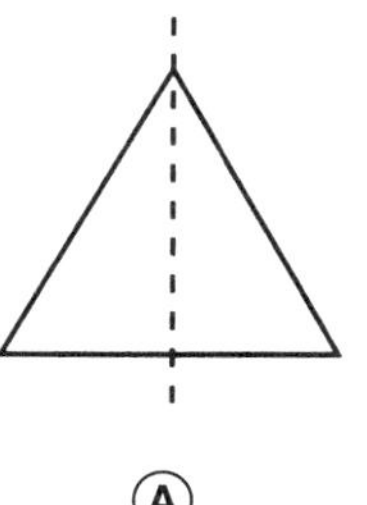	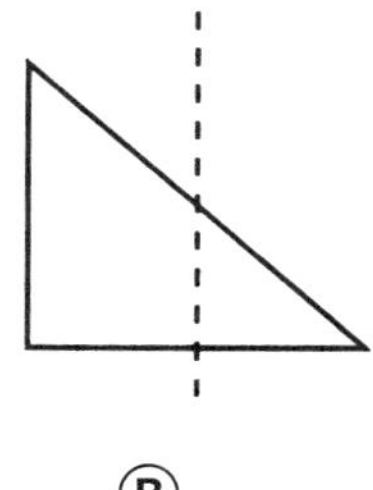	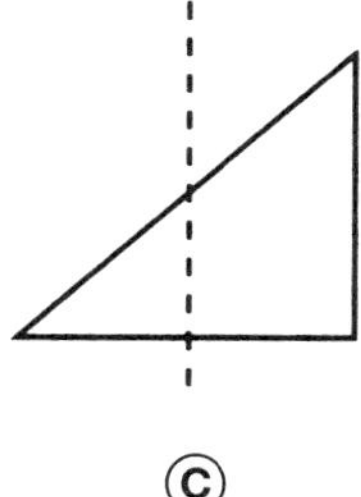	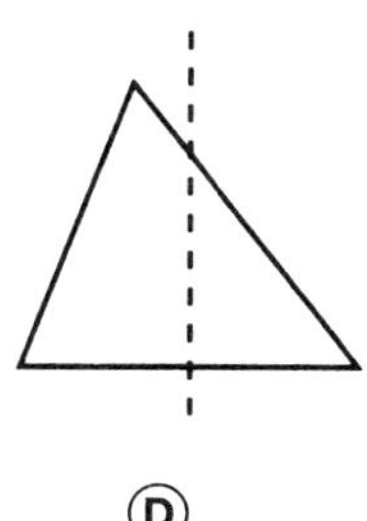
Ⓐ	Ⓑ	Ⓒ	Ⓓ

14 Look at the figure in the box. What word matches the figure?

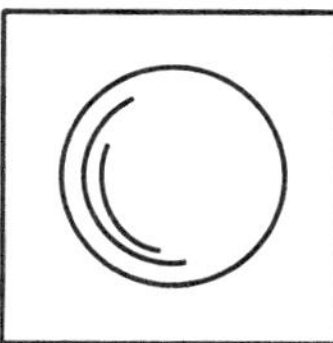

cube	sphere	pyramid	cone
Ⓕ	Ⓖ	Ⓗ	Ⓙ

GO

15 Ruth is twelve years old. Eli is four years older. How much older is Eli? Choose the correct number sentence.

Ⓐ $12 - 4 = \square$

Ⓑ $4 \times 12 = \square$

Ⓒ $4 + 12 = \square$

Ⓓ $12 \div 4 = \square$

16 A bicycle costs \$78. The lock costs \$12. How much do both cost? Choose the correct number sentence.

Ⓕ $\square + \$12 = \$78$

Ⓖ $\$12 + \square = \$78$

Ⓗ $\$78 - \square = \$12$

Ⓙ $\$78 + \$12 = \square$

17 If a taxi ride costs \$8, how much will it cost two people if they share a cab?

Ⓐ \$4

Ⓑ \$8

Ⓒ \$10

Ⓓ \$16

18 A baseball team has 20 players, 3 coaches, and 1 manager. How many people in all are part of the baseball team? Choose the right number sentence.

Ⓕ $20 - 3 - 1 = \square$

Ⓖ $20 + 3 + 1 = \square$

Ⓗ $20 + 3 = \square + 1$

Ⓙ $\square + 20 = 3 + 1$

19 A bag of chicken feed weighs 100 pounds. During May, Tina used 46 pounds of feed. How many pounds of feed did she have left? Pick the right number sentence.

Ⓐ $46 - \square = 100$

Ⓑ $\square - 100 = 46$

Ⓒ $100 - 46 = \square$

Ⓓ $\square + 100 = 46$

20 There are 22 students in Mr. Hill's class. Each student spends 4 hours a week at the computer. How much time in all do the students spend at the computer in a week?

Ⓕ 26 hours

Ⓖ 88 hours

Ⓗ 18 hours

Ⓙ 44 hours

21 A fence is 36 feet long. It is divided into 4 sections. How long is each section of fence?

Ⓐ 12 feet

Ⓑ 4 feet

Ⓒ 6 feet

Ⓓ 9 feet

STOP

Answer Key

Reading
Unit 1,
Word Analysis
Lesson 1–pg. 12

A	A
B	H
1	A
2	H
3	B
4	H
5	D
6	G
7	A
8	H

Lesson 2–pg. 13

A	C
B	G
1	A
2	G
3	A
4	F
5	C

Lesson 3–pg. 14

A	C
B	F
1	C
2	F
3	D
4	G
5	B
6	F

Lesson 4–pg. 15

A	C
B	F
C	A
D	G
1	B
2	F
3	C
4	G
5	C
6	G
7	C
8	G
9	C
10	G
11	C
12	F

Lesson 5–pg. 16

A	B
B	F
1	D
2	F
3	C
4	H
5	B
6	F
7	B
8	J

Lesson 6–pg. 17

A	D
B	H
1	A
2	G
3	B
4	H
5	D
6	H
7	A
8	G

Lesson 7–pgs. 18–21

E1	B
E2	F
E3	D
E4	H
E5	C
E6	G
E7	B
E8	H
1	C
2	F
3	B
4	F
5	C
6	J
7	B
8	H
9	A
10	G
11	A
12	H
13	A
14	G
15	A
16	H
17	C
18	F
19	C
20	F
21	D
22	G
23	A
24	G
25	A
26	G
27	C
28	F
29	C
30	F
31	B
32	F
33	B
34	G
35	A
36	H

Unit 2,
Vocabulary
Lesson 8–pg. 22

A	C
B	F
1	D
2	F
3	C
4	G

Lesson 9–pg. 23

A	B
B	H
1	C
2	J
3	C
4	F
5	D
6	G

Lesson 10–pg. 24

A	B
B	J
1	D
2	H
3	A
4	G
5	D
6	G

Lesson 11–pg. 25

A	D
B	F
1	C
2	G
3	A
4	J
5	B
6	J

Lesson 12–pg. 26

A	B
B	F
1	D
2	H
3	C
4	F
5	D
6	G

Lesson 13–pg. 27

A	D
B	J
1	B
2	F
3	D
4	H
5	B

Lesson 14–pgs. 28–31

E1	B
E2	J
E3	B
E4	H
E5	C
E6	F
E7	D
1	A
2	H
3	D
4	G
5	C
6	F
7	A
8	J
9	B
10	H
11	C
12	G
13	D
14	F
15	C
16	G
17	A
18	H
19	C
20	G
21	D
22	F
23	B
24	J
25	C
26	F
27	B
28	H
29	B
30	J

Unit 3,
Reading Comprehension
Lesson 15–pg. 32

A	B
1	C

2	F
3	D
4	G
5	D
6	H

Lesson 16–pg. 33

A	D
1	C
2	G
3	A
4	J

Lesson 17–pg. 34–37

A	A
1	C
2	G
3	B
4	F
5	C
6	H
7	D
8	G
9	A
10	H
11	A
12	G
13	C
14	F

Lesson 18–pgs. 38–41

A	C
1	C
2	F
3	D
4	H
5	D
6	F
7	B
8	H
9	A
10	J
11	B
12	F
13	B
14	H
15	C

Unit 4,
Test Practice
Part 1–pgs. 44–47

E1	C
E2	J
E3	A
E4	G
E5	B
E6	H
E7	B
E8	G
E9	D
1	A
2	G
3	A
4	H
5	B
6	J
7	C
8	G
9	C
10	F
11	A
12	F
13	C
14	G
15	A
16	G
17	A
18	G
19	C
20	F
21	C
22	J
23	B
24	F
25	A
26	H
27	C
28	G
29	A
30	H
31	C
32	G
33	D
34	G
35	C
36	F
37	B
38	H
39	A
40	J
41	B

Part 2–pgs. 48–53

E1	C
E2	G
E3	A
E4	F
E5	A
E6	J
E7	C
1	D
2	F
3	A
4	H
5	B
6	H
7	A
8	G
9	D
10	H
11	A
12	G
13	C
14	J
15	A
16	H
17	A
18	J
19	B
20	J
21	A
22	G
23	B
24	H
25	A
26	H
27	A
28	H
29	B
30	J
31	A
32	G
33	D
34	G
35	B
36	F
37	B
38	H
39	A
40	J
41	D
42	G
43	B
44	F
45	C
46	G
47	A

Part 3–pgs. 54–58

E1	B
E2	J
1	A
2	J
3	B
4	H
5	A
6	G
7	C
8	G
9	B
10	H
11	C
12	J
13	A
14	G
15	B
16	G
17	C
18	H
19	D

Language
Unit 1,
Listening
Lesson 1–pg. 60

A	B
1	B
2	F
3	B
4	H

Lesson 2–pg. 61

A	A
B	H
1	C
2	H
3	A
4	J
5	B
6	F

Lesson 3–pg. 62

E1	B
E2	H
1	C
2	H
3	A
4	G
5	D
6	F

Unit 2,
Language Mechanics
Lesson 4–pg. 63

A	D
B	G
C	B
1	A
2	H
3	D
4	F
5	C
6	G

Lesson 5–pg. 64

A	D
B	F
C	B
1	C
2	J
3	B
4	G
5	A
6	H

Lesson 6–pgs. 65–66

A	D
B	G
C	A
1	C
2	F

3	C
4	F
5	D
6	H
7	D
8	G
9	A

Lesson 7–pgs. 67–70

E1	B
E2	H
E3	C
E4	F
E5	C
E6	G
E7	B
E8	J
E9	D
1	D
2	F
3	C
4	G
5	A
6	F
7	B
8	H
9	D
10	G
11	A
12	G
13	A
14	H
15	B
16	F
17	A
18	H
19	A
20	J
21	C
22	J
23	B
24	J
25	A

Unit 3,
Language Expression
Lesson 8–pgs. 71–72

A	B
B	J
C	B
1	B
2	F
3	C
4	J
5	C
6	H
7	B
8	F
9	B
10	F
11	B
12	H

Lesson 9–pgs. 73–74

A	D
B	F
C	A
D	G
1	C
2	G
3	D
4	F
5	C
6	F
7	B
8	H
9	A
10	G

Lesson 10–pgs. 75–76

A	D
1	B
2	F
3	C
4	F
5	B
6	H

Lesson 11–pgs. 77–79

E1	A
E2	H
E3	A
E4	G
E5	B
1	B
2	G
3	A
4	G
5	A
6	J
7	C
8	G
9	A
10	H
11	B
12	F
13	D
14	F
15	B

Unit 4,
Spelling
Lesson 12–pgs. 80–82

A	B
B	J
C	C
D	H
E	B
1	A
2	H
3	A
4	G
5	D
6	G
7	B
8	H
9	A
10	H
11	A
12	H
13	D
14	G
15	C
16	G
17	B
18	G
19	C
20	F

Lesson 13–pgs. 83-85

E1	C
E2	F
E3	A
E4	H
E5	C
1	D
2	G
3	A
4	H
5	A
6	J
7	B
8	F
9	D
10	G
11	C
12	F
13	B
14	H
15	C
16	F
17	C
18	G
19	A
20	G
21	B
22	H
23	A
24	F
25	C

Unit 5,
Study Skills
Lesson 14–pgs. 86–87

A	A
1	A
2	H
3	B
4	H
5	A
6	F
7	B

Lesson 15–pgs. 88–90

E1	C
1	C
2	F
3	B
4	F
5	B
6	H
7	B
8	G
9	C
10	H
11	A

Unit 6,
Test Practice
Part 1–pg. 93

E1	B
E2	J
1	B
2	F
3	C
4	G
5	B
6	H

Part 2–pgs. 94–97

E1	A
E2	H
E3	B
E4	J
E5	B
E6	F
E7	C
E8	F
E9	B
1	B
2	F
3	D
4	G
5	C
6	F
7	C
8	F
9	C
10	H
11	D
12	G
13	C
14	F
15	C
16	F
17	A
18	J
19	B
20	F
21	C

22 J
23 C
24 J
25 A

Part 3–pgs. 98–101

E1 D
E2 G
E3 B
E4 H
E5 D
1 A
2 H
3 B
4 J
5 A
6 H
7 C
8 F
9 A
10 G
11 B
12 H
13 B
14 F
15 C
16 H
17 A
18 G

Part 4–pgs. 102–104

E1 C
E2 J
E3 C
E4 J
E5 A
1 B
2 F
3 C
4 H
5 A
6 G
7 A
8 F
9 D
10 H
11 B
12 H
13 A
14 G
15 A
16 H
17 B
18 J
19 A
20 H
21 B
22 F
23 B
24 F
25 C

Part 5–pgs. 105–106

E1 C
1 A
2 H
3 B
4 F
5 B
6 F
7 C
8 G

Math
Unit 1,
Concepts
Lesson 1–pgs. 108–109

A C
1 A
2 H
3 C
4 H
5 C
6 G
7 A
8 J
9 B

Lesson 2–pgs. 110–111

A B
1 A
2 H
3 D
4 G
5 A
6 H
7 B
8 J
9 C
10 G

Lesson 3–pgs. 112–113

A D
1 B
2 J
3 C
4 J
5 D
6 F
7 D
8 G
9 A

Lesson 4–pgs. 114–115

A D
1 B
2 F
3 C
4 G
5 A
6 J
7 C
8 G

Lesson 5–pgs. 116–119

E1 D
1 C
2 F
3 C
4 F
5 B
6 H
7 D
8 F
9 B
10 H
11 D
12 F
13 C
14 H
15 B
16 H
17 B
18 F
19 D
20 G

Unit 2,
Computation
Lesson 6–pgs. 120–121

A B
B F
1 D
2 F
3 D
4 G
5 D
6 H
7 D
8 F
9 B
10 F
11 A
12 H
13 D
14 H

Lesson 7–pgs. 122–123

A A
B J
1 C
2 J
3 B
4 G
5 A
6 J
7 C
8 G
9 D
10 G
11 B
12 F
13 D
14 G

Lesson 8–pg. 124

A B
B H
1 D
2 G
3 A
4 G
5 D
6 H

Lesson 9–pgs. 125–126

E1 C
E2 F
1 A
2 H
3 D
4 G
5 B
6 H
7 D
8 H
9 B
10 F
11 A
12 G
13 C
14 J
15 C
16 G
17 A
18 H

Unit 3,
Applications
Lesson 10–pgs. 127–129

A B
1 D
2 F
3 C
4 F
5 C
6 G
7 C
8 G
9 C
10 J
11 A
12 F

Lesson 11–pgs. 130–134

A B
1 B
2 H
3 D

4	F
5	B
6	J
7	A
8	H
9	A
10	G
11	D
12	H
13	B
14	G
15	D
16	H
17	A
18	G
19	D
20	F
21	B

Lesson 12–pgs. 135–138

A	C
1	A
2	H
3	D
4	G
5	D
6	H
7	A
8	G
9	C
10	F
11	B
12	F
13	D
14	H
15	C
16	F
17	B
18	J
19	B
20	F
21	C
22	J

Lesson 13–pgs. 139–144

E1	D
1	C
2	J
3	A
4	G
5	D
6	F
7	C
8	G
9	B
10	J
11	D
12	F
13	D
14	H
15	A
16	J
17	A
18	H
19	B
20	G

Unit 4,
Test Practice
Part 1–pgs. 145–148

E1	C
1	A
2	J
3	B
4	J
5	A
6	H
7	A
8	J
9	B
10	G
11	B
12	F
13	D
14	H
15	D
16	G
17	A
18	H
19	B

Part 2–pgs. 149–150

E1	D
E2	F
1	C
2	F
3	A
4	J
5	B
6	H
7	B
8	F
9	D
10	H
11	A
12	J
13	C
14	H
15	D
16	F
17	B
18	G

Part 3–pgs. 151–154

E1	C
1	A
2	H
3	D
4	G
5	C
6	J
7	A
8	G
9	A
10	H
11	A
12	J
13	A
14	G
15	C
16	J
17	A
18	G
19	C
20	G
21	D

Reading Progress Chart

Circle your score for each lesson. Connect your scores to see how well you are doing.

Unit 1	Lesson 1	8 7 6 5 4 3 2 1
	Lesson 2	5 4 3 2 1
	Lesson 3	6 5 4 3 2 1
	Lesson 4	12 11 10 9 8 7 6 5 4 3 2 1
	Lesson 5	8 7 6 5 4 3 2 1
	Lesson 6	8 7 6 5 4 3 2 1
	Lesson 7	36 35 34 33 32 31 30 29 28 27 26 25 24 23 22 21 20 19 18 17 16 15 14 13 12 11 10 9 8 7 6 5 4 3 2 1
Unit 2	Lesson 8	4 3 2 1
	Lesson 9	6 5 4 3 2 1
	Lesson 10	6 5 4 3 2 1
	Lesson 11	6 5 4 3 2 1
	Lesson 12	6 5 4 3 2 1
	Lesson 13	5 4 3 2 1
	Lesson 14	30 29 28 27 26 25 24 23 22 21 20 19 18 17 16 15 14 13 12 11 10 9 8 7 6 5 4 3 2 1
Unit 3	Lesson 15	6 5 4 3 2 1
	Lesson 16	4 3 2 1
	Lesson 17	14 13 12 11 10 9 8 7 6 5 4 3 2 1
	Lesson 18	15 14 13 12 11 10 9 8 7 6 5 4 3 2 1

Language Progress Chart

Circle your score for each lesson. Connect your scores to see how well you are doing.

Unit 1			Unit 2				Unit 3							
Lesson 1	Lesson 2	Lesson 3	Lesson 4	Lesson 5	Lesson 6	Lesson 7	Lesson 8	Lesson 9	Lesson 10	Lesson 11	Lesson 12	Lesson 13	Lesson 14	Lesson 15
4 3 2 1	6 5 4 3 2 1	6 5 4 3 2 1	6 5 4 3 2 1	6 5 4 3 2 1	9 8 7 6 5 4 3 2 1	25 24 23 22 21 20 19 18 17 16 15 14 13 12 11 10 9 8 7 6 5 4 3 2 1	12 11 10 9 8 7 6 5 4 3 2 1	10 9 8 7 6 5 4 3 2 1	6 5 4 3 2 1	15 14 13 12 11 10 9 8 7 6 5 4 3 2 1	20 19 18 17 16 15 14 13 12 11 10 9 8 7 6 5 4 3 2 1	25 24 23 22 21 20 19 18 17 16 15 14 13 12 11 10 9 8 7 6 5 4 3 2 1	7 6 5 4 3 2 1	11 10 9 8 7 6 5 4 3 2 1

Math Progress Chart

Circle your score for each lesson. Connect your scores to see how well you are doing.

Unit 1	Lesson 1	9, 8, 7, 6, 5, 4, 3, 2, 1
	Lesson 2	10, 9, 8, 7, 6, 5, 4, 3, 2, 1
	Lesson 3	9, 8, 7, 6, 5, 4, 3, 2, 1
	Lesson 4	8, 7, 6, 5, 4, 3, 2, 1
	Lesson 5	20, 19, 18, 17, 16, 15, 14, 13, 12, 11, 10, 9, 8, 7, 6, 5, 4, 3, 2, 1
Unit 2	Lesson 6	14, 13, 12, 11, 10, 9, 8, 7, 6, 5, 4, 3, 2, 1
	Lesson 7	14, 13, 12, 11, 10, 9, 8, 7, 6, 5, 4, 3, 2, 1
	Lesson 8	6, 5, 4, 3, 2, 1
	Lesson 9	18, 17, 16, 15, 14, 13, 12, 11, 10, 9, 8, 7, 6, 5, 4, 3, 2, 1
Unit 3	Lesson 10	12, 11, 10, 9, 8, 7, 6, 5, 4, 3, 2, 1
	Lesson 11	21, 20, 19, 18, 17, 16, 15, 14, 13, 12, 11, 10, 9, 8, 7, 6, 5, 4, 3, 2, 1
	Lesson 12	22, 21, 20, 19, 18, 17, 16, 15, 14, 13, 12, 11, 10, 9, 8, 7, 6, 5, 4, 3, 2, 1
	Lesson 13	20, 19, 18, 17, 16, 15, 14, 13, 12, 11, 10, 9, 8, 7, 6, 5, 4, 3, 2, 1

STUDENT NOTES

STUDENT NOTES

STUDENT NOTES

STUDENT NOTES

STUDENT NOTES

STUDENT NOTES